FRANCIS MACNAB

The
HUMAN SPIRIT

Inner
strength
in
turbulent
times

crown
content

Published by
Crown Content
A.C.N. 096 393 636
A.B.N. 37 096 393 636
75 Flinders Lane
Melbourne Vic. 3000
Telephone: (03) 9654 2800
Fax: (03) 9650 5261
Internet: www.crowncontent.com.au
Email: mail@crowncontent.com.au

The National Library of Australia
Cataloguing-in-Publication entry:

Macnab, Francis, 1931-.
    The human spirit : inner strength in turbulent times.

    ISBN 1 86350 398 6

    1. Spirituality. 2. Anxiety - Religious aspects -
Christianity. I. Title.

248.4

Cover & Page Design: Ben Graham

Printed in Australia by Brown Prior Anderson

"Things may be the same again; and we must fight.
Not in the hope of winning, but rather of keeping
Something alive."

Henry Reed

Contents

THE HUMAN SPIRIT

Preface

Long before that day that will be forever known as September 11, human spirits were under strain. But, after that day, the worldwide human spirit would be vital to the way individual people and large populations would cope. How would the human spirit respond to such a catastrophe, and the pervasive horror and fear which followed?

Many called on the wells of their religion. Other asked why God would let such a dreadful evil happen. The fragility and chaos of the human spirit were suddenly and frighteningly exposed. We realized that this was not a faceless evil, but the work of men with powerful beliefs and absolute and ultimate convictions. Any idea of an intervening God, watching from a place called heaven, became little more than a regressive fantasy.

Rumor and fear, distrust and hate, shock and impulses of outrage, showed human beings with insubstantial resources to meet the future in an insightful or integrated way.

We had been travelling on "low to empty" for more than a generation. Anxiety and depression had become accepted as modern epidemics. Their symptoms were treated without any specific examination of their underlying spiritual pathology or their cultural and interpersonal alienation.

Cancer and heart disease have continued to kill large numbers, and only recently have research studies begun to show that these, too, may have concealed components of social deprivation and despair of the spirit.

Distressing events and traumas have all too commonly left personalities deeply wounded and in emotional pain – without effective healing or consolation. In the workplace, discontent, stress and burnout have blighted ordinary expectations and possibilities of inspiration and joy. And so the circle of social malaise widens and the strength of the human spirit is continually tested

Within many parts of christian religion there has been a strange contentment with empty churches and an irrelevant faith. In some parts there has been an enthusiasm for fundamentalism and a mindless acceptance of authoritarian religion. This is regardless of their evasion of an intelligent scrutiny of the scriptures and their totalitarian moral absolutes and exclusive attitudes and postures.

People speak loosely of the human spirit – how we all need to have strong spirits, generous spirits, and good spirits. But what are the qualities of the human spirit? What part do they play in life events. How are these qualities sustained or reconstructed after they have been exhausted?

A reassessment of what spirituality means urgently awaits us. We need to discover how a thorough-going contemporary interpretation of religion and belief systems can become constructive components for our health and well-being, for acceptance of differences, and for the things that bring us together in our deepest humanity.

We are, even after our best and worst events, one people – travelling on different pathways, and all in search of those glimpses of a divine presence that will enrich our personal lives and lift us to be better human beings.

The human spirit may be wounded and injured. It may be deprived and alienated and subjected to generations of violence, discrimination and injustice. It may wither into ineffectiveness.

The response of the human spirit may be anger and violence, anxiety and self-destruction, apathy, helplessness and depression.

But the human spirit can realize there are different responses to the strain. It can learn compassion and kindness, collaboration and communal bonding, and purpose. It can join with other processes and people in recovery and resilience, in thriving in spite of pain and transcending its pain. We are recognizing that the human spirit needs our urgent and constant attention and care.

The Pains Of Our Vulnerability

The Lessons That Follow

E ver since September 11, 2001, we have heard it many times – we have said it many times – "The world has changed. A new vulnerability has invaded the world."

We have always been vulnerable; a few years ago we were vulnerable to nuclear warfare. In more recent times we were vulnerable to the collapse of the economies and even today to the possible collapse of large and trusted companies. Each one of us and every family is vulnerable every day to problems that can't be resolved or to illnesses for which there is no cure. We have always been vulnerable. But since September 11, the world has changed drastically as we discover that we have no adequate defences against the invading enemy and the old and well-tried protections no longer work.

In the Old Testament, we had the account of King David dying. He was not yet dead when Adonijah declared himself king – a take-over without negotiation. But David outwitted him by quickly declaring his own Solomon as king. Adonijah knew his number was up. He seized on the old and tried strategy of security and safety by rushing to the altar and holding on to the horns of the altar. But would it work? He knew that Solomon's troopers could quickly cut him down. It could not save him, not for long anyway, and he knew it. (1 Kings 1:1-34)

The frightening concern is not our naked vulnerability because we were always vulnerable, and hoping we were not. The frightening concern is what do we do when our vulnerability is so drastically exposed?

We have – as people, groups and individuals – chosen to block ourselves off from our own psychology: the psychology of our ever-present vulnerability and the psychology of the appropriate response. We are heavily wedded to materialistic politics –

- Caring for the aged is all about hospitals, nursing homes and beds, and very little about the psychology of keeping people healthy and emotionally alive

- Planning for retirement and the future is about money and financial planning, and very little about psychology of life-span vitality

- Education is about schools, performance and job training, and very little about psychology of relationships, the psychology of prejudice or the psychology of love and hate, of collaboration and fear, or the psychology of life-skills.

In our various vulnerabilities, we need to study carefully the best response – in advance – lest it all happens and we are unprepared and unskilled.

The Pentagon in Washington was surely regarded as the nation's horns on the altar. Nobody would dare touch it – it was the very symbol of the armed fortress. But one event has done two things –

- It ploughed a hole in the walls as big as a football field

- It has suddenly introduced an enemy that is "not human but ghostly, flickering here and there on the faces of nearly 20,000 Pentagon employees who once thought their building was untouchable..."(*Time Magazine*, Oct 15, 2001 p.67)

The ghostly presence is anxiety and fear. Before September 11, the Pentagon did not have a single full-time working psychologist. Today, there are nearly a hundred, working around the clock to help people cope with their devastated lives. "It is the dawn of a new era," declared Andrew Goldstein of Washington. We have to find different responses to our realized vulnerability lest fear becomes the most disabling enemy of all.

This week I am to give an address on the unconscious mind – what goes on in the deeper parts of our mind and how can we understand it better? Many might say, "Who wants to? Leave it alone!" But when we refuse to understand our unconscious mind, it is out of our control – so we can't understand why people behave the way they do; what frightens them into hateful and destructive behavior? Who are we frightened of? I will use a dream, because our dreams sometimes help us understand our unconscious mind.

> *A man is in his house asleep. Suddenly, his baby son in the next room begins to cry. He goes in and picks the child up and walks it to and fro along the passageway. When the child is quiet he returns it to the cot only to find some stray cat is curled up asleep in the cot.*

> *He boots it out the door and then returns to put the baby down. But the baby is now screaming; and*

*when the father goes to straighten the cot, he finds
another cat is already there and has messed profusely
over all the cot clothing. He wakes up.*

That's a dream. The man who had the dream is a
man whose children are adults living away from home.
There is no cot in his house. The dream, however,
disturbed him for days. What was it about – and what
will be his response to it? It tells us about a conflict in
the man's mind; and although he may forget the dream,
or be unconcerned about its meaning, the conflict will
remain to affect his health and well-being, the sense of
who he is and what he will do in the future. He woke
up – but did he really wake up? What response will he
give to the trouble of his dream? Anger, panic, helplessness, despair? Fear explodes other fears.

The dream may give its lesson to anyone of us –
when we are least expecting it, something can invade
our lives, our space, our security, our self-confidence
and cause such a mess that we might have difficulty
making an effective response. When we are fully awake
to what is happening, what will be our **best** response
– and how will we measure the word "BEST"?

As we look at ourselves facing a new era in the world
of frightening possibilities it is worth remembering
that there have been two other world destabilizations
in recent history. One was back in the 1840s when the

Europe-dominated world went through an intellectual and spiritual upheaval, "that would leave nothing untouched and virtually everything changed" (John Barville). The "revaluation of all values" that Friederich Nietzsche had so passionately called for, came about – though in a different form from what he had wished.

And the second huge era of vulnerability – was the prolonged Cold War of the 50s through to the 70s where at any moment a nuclear war could have swept humanity and all living creatures into oblivion. Millions upon millions of dollars were spent on an enemy that may never have become an enemy if other ways had been explored.

But vulnerability comes at us from several directions affecting us on the world scale: in employment, in relationships, in physical and mental health, and the strength of our inner spirits.

The critical issue is not that we discover we are vulnerable, but knowing our vulnerability, what will be our response?

1. One of the major life-tasks is finding effective ways to control and manage the things that would threaten us. We know we cannot ever be completely safe, for although we might put deadlocks on all the doors and windows, these do not protect us from illness and disease. They do not protect us from the barbs of other people. They do not protect us from the external or natural disasters.

   Our life-tasks are to gain a sense of control over the things "out there" that threaten us. Often this will mean that you seek help, seek appropriate resources, or some valued intervention.

   The disciples of Jesus out there in the storm of life realized they were in difficulty. They sought help, to regain a sense of control over the events of their lives. (St Mark 4:35-41)

2. The first help that Jesus gave them focused on their fear. "You are too easily frightened," he said. Fear is a huge problem for all of us. The vital issue is what is the response to make? The disciples were frantic. Adonijah in the Old Testament was terrified.

   All of them were facing life-threatening situations. Jesus spoke of getting control of fear. It is a very spontaneous response to want to respond in ways that destroy the source of your fear. But fear is elusive, often ubiquitous and very tyrannical.

At many levels in life we are taught never to show our fear – to keep ourselves strong and without any sign of weakness. If you believe that fear is a single, identifiable enemy, then you want to knock it out, and there are plenty of team players who cheer the troops.

But fear is a very diffuse enemy, a powerful killer and a destabilizing emotion. We need to learn ways to understand and control the fears that can –

- Send us into irrational responses

- Send us into rigid beliefs and destructive behavior

- Send us into illness and early death

- Send us into vast costs and still not provide a solution.

We need to intercept fear – and find effective ways to reduce its power.

3. Jesus did not have much of a solution for fear. He said, "You need faith."

    But faith in what? We look for faith in ultimate goodness. That is what he stood for. In spite of everything, keep alive your faith in ultimate goodness. In the old world we tried to overcome our insecurity by making ourselves so powerful that other people became insecure instead of us. In the old world we tried to believe that no stray cat would ever get into the baby's cot when our backs were turned. But then we discovered "the dreadful had already happened". (Heidegger) The cat's name was cancer. The cat's name was depression. The cat's name was self-sabotage. The cat's name was the neurosis of mass fear.

So, he said, you need faith. But faith in what? It's faith in ultimate goodness; faith that people everywhere, in vast numbers, are ready to salute and praise ultimate goodness. More and more people will be impatient with the hypocrisy of politicians and people dedicated to destruction and they will put on the coat of ultimate goodness and wear it as an expression of their faith. Jesus encouraged his disciples so that each person would encourage others to wear that jacket. When they do the whole world will become kin.

4. And notice one thing more – as Jesus was speaking, everything and everyone became calm. Our vulnerability is always difficult, but it has less power when there is a sense of calm.

We make better decisions. We are better to be with. And we find a better self being created in ourselves. I have often quoted those good words of Ainslie Meares –

"So we sit and are quiet
In the calm and the stillness
In the depth of it all is good in our heart
Sit quietly
For it is in the quietness that we grow."

The lesson that follows the pain of our vulnerability is to discover the best response to the awareness of our vulnerability. And the four sub-lessons are these

1. As far as possible, find ways to control and manage the invasive force that makes you vulnerable. Protect yourself whenever you can.

2. Focus on the fear. Intercept it – reduce it! Manage it.

3. Nurture your faith in ultimate goodness in spite of everything.

4. Cultivate a calmness and courage that works as a way of changing everything.

Spiritual Care is Vital

We All Need It

The Nazi gas ovens extinguished the lives of millions of innocent powerless men, women and children, and we only heard about it years after it had happened.

The Stalin Regime in Russia extinguished, it is believed, nearly 20 million of its people, and we only heard about it years after it happened.

The bomb on Hiroshima killed hundreds of thousands of people, and we heard about it after it happened.

The earthquake in Turkey buried 10,000 people and we heard about it after it happened.

But the horrific event in New York happened while we watched it happen. I was in Tokyo. We had returned from an outing and came home and discovered we were just in time to watch the late news. We saw it all as it was happening. That was horrific; but some of our friends were right there as the dreadful event took place in front of them.

At times of great tragedy and horrifying circumstances we need more than the heroic work of the rescuers; we need more than the words of politicians and the preachers. We need that vital spiritual care to help us embrace the vast reality that we are living in a different world. We expected people to behave in the way we expected or wanted them to behave, but globalization, and all that has come with it, has changed that. A new reality is upon us.

I was in Britain and watched on television each morning at 8.30, as roman catholic children were led to school through a protestant neighborhood, while protestant crowds jeered and shouted abuse, and one threw a blast bomb. Christian protestants and christian catholics in the same city and the same neighborhood, and the ultimate target – children under the age of 10. They were led to school each morning by the catholic priest in cassock. They could have gone the long way round, but instead claimed the right and chose confrontation with the most appalling behavior of their fellow human beings claiming to be protestants. At times of such dreadful behavior we need more than soldiers and police, more than the words of archbishops and moderators. We need a vital spiritual care that will exceed the failure of spiritual care that has been long since lost to the institutional church kind of religion – something that transcends the divisions and empty rhetoric of religions.

We can call people suicidal maniacs; we can call them fundamental fanatics; we can call them crazy individuals; we can call them terrorists; we can call them name after name, but it does not deal with the frightening fact that some people have different belief systems. Some people will fight and die for their cause; some people believe they are living in an unjust world and will go to extremes to let their case be recognized. You can call it evil if you like. But evil exists in human behavior, and human behavior can arise out of the most powerful motivations. And suddenly the most powerful nation in the world becomes powerless in the face of the power of beliefs arising out of a very different world-view than we have tried to understand.

As I left Tokyo airport on Thursday evening, I noticed that the Japanese middle-aged man next to me – far better dressed than I was – closed his eyes and raised his hands in prayer as the plane prepared for take-off. After we rose into the air, our eyes met for just a moment, and I wondered how many of us in our Christian tradition have bothered spending many moments understanding anything about the Shinto religion? How many of us have already developed some kind of evasion about Islamic religion that we are astonished – as I was – to discover what the Turks (for example) feel about life and the world and human values.

Our view of God and our religion has become so ineffective and outdated, that, sadly, at the memorial service in Washington, they brought Billy Graham to give the address. And he showed in one sentence that he was still clinging to an outdated view of the world, and an outdated view of God, when he asked the question, "Why does God let such evil happen?"

As if God is up there in the sky keeping watch over the people in the World Trade Centre, who tragically became the suffering victims of human behavior motivated by a completely different theology and world view. And while politicians talk about globalization and economics, nobody is talking about spiritual care and the conversations that need to take place between people of different religions and world-views. Spiritual care: that brings a different conception of God.

I brought here last year some of the discussions of *A Parliament of Minds*. (Univ. of N.Y. Press, 2000).

Robert Müller, for many years Assistant Secretary General of the United Nations, and regarded as the "father of global education", said this –

> "The religions say, 'I am the truth', and they are ready to kill each other for the truth which, in the end, is practically the same in all the religions."

> And now, "let me tell you what I observed in the UN. The first one is that humans, from a physical point of view, have globalized themselves to an incredible degree: television, microscopes, communication, travel..."

> "Physical abilities of the human person have been multiplied in an incredible way and that created a new physical global species. The same has happened in the mental field. We have today a global brain ... But then comes the heart. Now that! We do not have a global heart. In the UN, I never hear the word love in a speech. Love is outer, something strange ... (What about) love of nature, the love of peace, love for humans, and love for the planet... And then it comes to the soul, which is the highest love of all. We have a soul where we can each obtain an inner answer by saying, 'I'm part of a mysterious universe. I'm glad to be alive. My life is a miracle, and I have to be a good person as a human being.' And this, in international affairs, is almost totally absent. We need a global soul."

There is a spiritual care that is vital to help people around the world understand the global soul that will truly "bind-up the broken-hearted, proclaim liberty to the captives, that will bring gladness instead of the mourners tears, and a garment of hope to those who are heavy of heart". (Isaiah, chapter 61)

The other day I watched my daughter's two-year-old do what two-year-olds have done through the generations. He built his blocks into a high tower, and proudly, joyfully, sat back admiring them. But his four-year-old sister put an end to that. With one swish, the tower was scattered across the floor. An immediate retaliation took place – the two-year-old running wild, knocking over everything he could. A fight ensued with both screaming, and soon even their mother had to shout to restore some peace. It happened on the day the New York Towers fell. In its telling way, it reminds us all that, though we rightly feel someone has to be taught that some behavior will not be tolerated, how that is done might determine whether we will embrace a way of enhancing our humanness rather than diminishing it. For that, too, is a vital expression of spiritual care. So: spiritual care is vital –

1. To embrace that vast reality that we are living in a different world.

2. To realize that a new and better spiritual care is needed that exceeds religious emptiness and religious violence.

3. To understand different ways of understanding the human scene and our view of God.

4. To bring our attention for the need of a global soul that will listen to the need of the refugee, and the hungry, the despised.

5. To help human beings realize the precious value of human life and the need to search for a better humanity.

So, the Bible said, three things remain. Just three – faith, hope and charity. These three sit at the heart of all spiritual care – faith, hope and charity – ancient words originating 500 years BC, from the Greek philosopher Heraclitus, and put into the christian context of St Paul. Ancient they may be, but their practical expression may well contribute to ways of transcending the violence and prejudice, and misunderstandings, and suffering that we witness. They can be just words. They can get lost in religious rhetoric, or they can become part of everyone's consciousness, regardless of religious involvement.

Faith, hope and love can take a tangible expression to change the way we cope with our personal experience and to help us deal with the mammoth tragedies of our day.

Faith is about the commitment of the human heart, and the beliefs that go to shape our attitudes and behavior.

Hope is sustaining the courage to hold on in spite of the worst circumstances. Hope holds aloft the symbols of life. Hope is seen in the symbol of Mingary.

Charity is about forming bonds. It is about caring beyond the tax deduction. It is about humans reaching humans with a desire to understand and help and care. Charity sometimes needs to be forced by the courts of justice; but, ultimately, charity shows humanity striving towards a better humanity.

Amitai Etzioni in his article on "The Good Society" wrote –

> *"When it comes to material goods, enough is never enough (I do not argue) in favor of a life of sack cloth, of poverty and self-denial. The argument is that once basic material needs are well sated and securely provided for, additional income does not add to happiness. Hard evidence shows that profound contentment is in nourishing relationships, in bonding with others, in community building, in cultural and spiritual pursuits."* (Futurist July-August 2001, p.68)

Or take the words of American Republican Senator Mark Hatfield. As a young man, he was a naval officer deeply involved in the war against Japan. After the war, in September 1945, he was part of the crew that went into Hiroshima about a month after the bomb was dropped.

> *"There was a smell to the city – and total silence. It was amazing to see the utter and indiscriminate devastation in every direction."*

As they sailed into the canals, Japanese parents and their children watched silently.

> *"When we landed, the kids saw we weren't going to kill them, so they began to gather around. We realized they were hungry so we took our lunches and broke them up and gave them to as many kids as we could."*

Senator Hatfield said –

> *"You learn to hate with passion in wartime. If you didn't kill your enemy, they'll kill you. But sharing those sandwiches with the people who had been my enemy was sort of therapy for me. I could almost feel my hate leaving me. It was almost a spiritual experience."* (see Brokaw, T (ed). The Greatest Generation, Delta, 1998)

In this simple act, he was living out the meaning of those words so vital to spiritual care for every transition and tragedy of life. We all need words to touch the deepest parts of our soul – words that help us live through our experiences and transcend their pain and anxiety. When so many things can so easily undermine our courage....

There are three things that last forever: faith hope and charity. But the greatest of them is charity: a charity of the bonds of human caring; a charity that lifts us all to feel part of a better humanity and a life that feels worthwhile.

Become Bearers of Worthwhile Spiritual Values

Recently, my eye fell on an article in one of the British Psychological Journals. It was called "Bearers of Spiritual Values," written by an academic from Oxford University. It began –

> "My research looked at the social roles of two distinct groups in 19th century English society: women and clergymen ... At different times, each group was regarded with special reverence, provided it kept to its 'proper sphere', and did not interfere with real life. Each group, at different times, was required by the

> *rest of society to function as bearers of its moral and spiritual values."* (The Psychologist, Jan 1991, p.25)

We do not live in 19th century England. Right now, most of us would have difficulty saying who are the bearers of our moral and spiritual values. Furthermore, we would have even greater difficulty naming those moral and spiritual values that we would regard as needing bearers to contain them, to confirm them and to convey them across society and to a future generation.

We can readily recognize the values that have been around us for some time – the values of personal gain and aggrandizement; the values of pushing for prestige and powerful possibilities; the values of aggressive and divisive living; the values of sectional favors and gains. They were clearly present in the people of the New Testament story. Jesus visited the home of Simon, and while there, discovered an immoral, crazy woman crawling around the floor, kissing his feet, wetting them with tears, drying them with her hair. Embarrassing, crazy and terribly inappropriate for any cocktail or garden party where personal gain, prestige and power, aggressive, and "them and us" sentiments, were alive and well. But Jesus called Simon and said –

"You see this crazy, immoral woman?

Notice she really wants to grow into a new woman.

Notice how genuine she is.

Notice her generosity.

Notice you are concerned about how your head looks and she is crawling around our feet.

She reminds us not of life's parts, but of life's totality."

Here are worthwhile spiritual values -

- The values of human growth
- The values of authenticity
- The values of a softening generosity
- The values that embrace the totality of things!

1. Sometimes the people we expect to be the bearers of the really important values of life are not the best bearers at all. At the time, we thought we had our cameras pointed right at them – the bearers of the important values – but when we developed the film, it was BLANK!

   Let's start with the photographs. The Gulf War placed the King of Jordan in an extremely difficult position. He wanted to remain friends with America, but then he lived right next door to Iraq, and Jordan's Port of Aqabar serves as Iraq's major access to the sea.

Some American newspapers were unsympathetic to the Jordan king's attempt to be neutral. *Newsweek* published a photograph of the king captioned, "Brotherly esteem: King Hussein presents a rifle to Saddam." The photograph showed the king holding a rifle out to his Arab colleague in a moment of comradeship. The reader was left to assume that while he claimed to work for peace, the king was smilingly giving Saddam weapons.

> *"A little checking, which 'Newsweek' apparently did not do, would have revealed that the photograph was made some years before the crisis began, when Iraq was at war with Iran and was still on our side. The rifle in the king's hands is a Mauser K-98 of WWII vintage, which had originally been given to the king's grandfather ... in 1948, by the Iraqi army. The photo was taken when King Hussein, well-known as a rifle collector, presented the rifle to Saddam Hussein to be placed in the Baghdad museum."* (Christian Century M27, 1991)

We might have expected better than this; but without any checks, the people we expect to be the bearers of really important values are not the best bearers at all.

I have already mentioned the clergy. There was a time when people would say, "Well, he is a clergyman, he must be all right." Now we know that we need to check what kind of clergy he/she is; what they really stand for; and what they are really up to.

We have seen only a fraction of the damage that extremists have done. We have seen the rorts carried out by fine-looking, well-dressed tele-evangelists. We have seen only a few of the human bodies spread out in streets and gardens, tortured and executed by people with strong commitments to one or other of the three religions that are probably best known to us: Christian, Judaism and Muslim.

In recent times, as the fires of republicanism have been stoked, some people have said that the royal family stands for values important to our society. There must be better arguments for retaining the royal family. After all, if we were looking for a model to encourage people to pay their taxes, the royal family would hardly qualify.

Who will be the bearers of the important values? Many would say –

"Of course! The parents." But parents have had a hard time communicating their values to their children, and their children are not listening.

Jesus said to Simon, in effect –

> *"Sometimes the people we expect to be the bearers of the really important values of life, are not the best bearers at all!"*

2. Sometimes the really good values of life come from rather unexpected sources.

> *"You see this immoral woman at my feet? She is saying more than all your outward pursuit of self-gain. She wants to grow. There is authenticity here. There is a softening generosity. There is a desire to embrace everything. These are really good values, Simon ... Sarah ... Samuel ... Susannah ... Saul ... Salome! All of you."*

How often people have told me that in their moment of need, help came not from all the expected people and the expected places, but from some unknown person playing a particular melody on the flute. Viktor Frankl, in a concentration camp, found his whole being transformed as a bird dropped down on a clod of earth in front of him.

For some, the great values of life do not come from people of high office, but from people like the physician Dr Janusz Korczak of the War-saw ghetto. He looked after the children and ultimately insisted that if they were to die in the gas ovens, he would die with them. The memorial in Treblinka to 840,000 people who died there consists of large rocks that mark the place. The rocks bear no inscriptions other than the name of the city or the country from which the victims came. One rock only bears a man's name. It reads, "Janusz Korczak and the children."

Sometimes the really good values come from unexpected places.

3. There is a need to reassess what the really good values are; and who will bear them and how they will bear them.

Keith Mason, a Sydney QC, has written an unusual book called, *Constancy and Change.* It is basically a book about the Australian legal system and how some things remain constant and how some parts of the law must change.

He recalls a great deal of the early settlement of the colony and how various people deter-mined what values would be important and how they would be communicated and sus-tained. One part of the book tells of Samuel Marsden, an early chaplain. He frequently was in conflict with Governor Macquarie. He strongly defended his rights and in order to do his part, he became a magistrate, and began the peculiar task of linking human law with God's justice. In 1823, Commissioner Biffe thought,

> *"Marsden had become hardened by the daily contemplation of crime and evil and that he resorted excessively to corporal punishment. Biffe saw the chaplain as having gradually lost that compassion 'which formed the ornament in the character and manners of a Christian Minister'."* (p.100).

Jonah, in the Old Testament, was given a task. Faced with the test and challenge of his life, he said, "I'm not ready for that", and headed in the other direction. Some people are like Jonah; they know what is required of them. But they say, "I'm not in that."

Jonah then had an experience that led him to reassess where he was headed and what values in life he would serve. His time in "the belly of the whale" was a poetic or imagery way of telling us that he had a very deep involutional experience that caused him to review everything. Faced with the demands of the task, he could have recoiled again from it, but the story picturesquely describes his being expelled from the whale. It indicated that sometimes we realize we can defer no longer – we must act.

Milan Kundera said –

> *"Human life occurs only once, and the reason why we cannot determine which of our decisions are good and which are bad is that in a given situation we can make only one decision. We are not granted a second, third, or fourth life in which to compare various decisions."*
> (The Unbearable Lightness of Being p.222)

In similar view, Stephen Grellet said in 1800 –

> *"I expect to pass through this world but once; any good thing therefore that I can do, or any kindness that I can show to any fellow-creature, let me do it now; let me not defer or neglect it, for I shall not pass this way again."*

4. Sometimes people give lip service to the really good values of life, but that's all. In fact, you can do two things at once – lip service and live the lie.

There is a problem for the defence strategies of a country. Should doctors and psychologists employ their skills to advise governments on how to get prisoners to yield up information? Some years ago the question was asked of the British prime minister if special interrogation procedures had been used. The prime minister gave an unequivocal assurance that was accepted by the community. But those with particular training in this area knew very well what the methods described, entailed. Lip service and the lie.

Jesus said in effect to Simon, "It would be easy to nod that you understand with your head what I have said – but this woman is not only acting with her head, she is embracing the totality of everything. It is not only a different way of doing business. She is embracing a different psychology. It is a psychology of healing of the past, and living authentically, and with a softening generosity toward the future. It is a total change of her psychology of living." As a bit of a joke we say here at St Michael's that we have several unofficial clubs. There is the club for all those who have had by-pass surgery. There is the club for hip replacements. There is the club for cataract surgery. Several people have told me that it was one thing to have their surgery, but then followed a complete change to their basic psychology.

Many other people here have very different experiences. Several of you who have experienced and endured the dreadful experiences of life – it was one thing, you said, to be part of that torture, or the trauma, or the loss – but you really started to grow again as you realized the need for a completely new psychology within you.

A psychology of release, of healing, of reconstruction. A psychology of growth, of rejoining the joy of things. A psychology of embracing the totality of things in a different way from ever before.

I read recently in *21C*, the magazine of the commission for the future, that the then Federal Minister, Mr Simon Crean, was asked – "By 2001, what are the key things Australia must have done to ensure its success as a country in the 21st century?"

He replied

> *"...the greatest task facing Australia is recognizing that the most important commodity in the 21st century will be knowledge, and the most important capability will be that of accessing, creating and using knowledge. Having and using knowledge will determine how well nations will adapt, survive and prosper in a global environment characterized by accelerating change and increasing uncertainty."*

Now I applaud the value of knowledge, but it is not the greatest task facing Australia. You can have all the knowledge in the world and be a tyrant; you can have all the knowledge in the world and be totally insensitive; you can have the knowledge and not know the things that belong to your peace.

The greatest task facing Australia is the need for a new psychology. It's the greatest task for all of us. There is no lip service or let-out. We need a psychology that releases us into our emerging identity; that gives us a readiness to become new bearers of the really good values of life.

Know Your Spiritual Qualities

Release Them For Your Health

The old and rusted ship hulk on the shoreline attracts us to it. Our mind quickly activates our imagination, as we see that vessel in its heyday confidently cutting through the ocean, its passengers and crew emanating their excitement and anticipation. That is the way many people describe their spiritual life – once like the ship sailing the high seas, now an empty, rusting hulk left behind on the shore.

How then can our spiritual qualities invigorate our mind and contribute to our health?

Many adults are very cautious in talking to their children about their spiritual pursuits, their spiritual values and their spiritual qualities. Perhaps they are afraid their children will ask them to say precisely what they are talking about. Perhaps they fear that their children will make that definitive separation by declaring that their parents are a bit odd – that they have a religious flea in their ear; that they are still hoping that the old rusted hulk on the shore line will sail again.

We have been poorly served by the church and conventional religion. They talked in a glib way about "spiritual things", somehow superior to the material things: that we – ordinary people – should feel sinful and guilty if we chose the material things of wealth, physical possessions, scientific and secular pursuits and the pleasures of the body. We were told that these were all under a shadow, whereas the spiritual life would lead to God's fuller acceptance.

Then the spiritual qualities were demonstrated as a praying piety, a pretense of holiness, an absorption in an attitude of sin and penitence often in some kind of synchrony with authoritarianism and concealed hostility. On top of that, this spirituality could effectively study the scriptures with intensity while harboring in their hearts large ventricles full of anger, self-righteousness and hubris.

It's a long way from that exhortation of the epistle to the Colossians – "above all, be loving, for love links us to fullness of life". Jesus looked at the fig tree. This tree had not blossomed or born any fruit. It was just taking up space. But the gardener in the parable said, "Let me feed it, let me give it one more opportunity to grow. Let us see if we can encourage new life."

Jesus was indicating that the physical presence of the tree was a given. It was there. But it had no purpose, no life, no fruit and no future. In this parable he was speaking to all of us!

We are all born with a physical body, into physical and material circumstances. But notice how parents act to bring life, vitality, and personality into their child. Notice how environments are selected to encourage best growth, best happiness and best health. If we miss out on that nurturing of the spirit, the spirit does not flourish. This child lacks something. This child is a good scholar but she is temperamental, often depressed and difficult. That child has excellent skills with his hands but lacks any real animation or excitement.

We are led to believe that millions of dollars of ecstasy pills were intercepted at Melbourne airport – their destination was to go straight into the bodies of young people to give their minds a tilt and their spirit a lift.

While we have been trying to come to some under-standing of the large populations of depression and the epidemic of drugs, we have not seen this as a disorder in our human spirits.

I know governments have called on the conservative wings of religion to reassert their ineffective, outdated beliefs. But what have they done except reiterate a religion that does not work? Try to cash a bank note from Romania over at the National Bank and they will tell you it has no value. Likewise, most of that pietistic religion has no conversion value when it comes to your psychological and physical health.

We all know that, at our best moments, when the human spirit is fully alive, we are in touch with our best humanity.

What we want are spiritual qualities that, when identified, will convert to enhance our mind and contribute to our health.

If we all thought our spiritual qualities were important for our health, for our community, why don't we form an institute for the development of the human spirit? If we all recognized the wide consequences of soul deadness, why don't we start saying, "it is not too late; let's nurture the fig tree". Give it a different opportunity to grow. Clearly we have to get past talking in religious mumbo jumbo, in pietistic rhetoric, and start seriously studying the impact of good spiritual qualities on health and well-being. These days, I believe theological colleges are nothing but a waste of people's money: producing clergy who are preoccupied with the rusty hulk on the seashore.

Instead, we look for a huge response from the people of the churches to say – "we need to know how to keep our spirits alive for our mind and health". If I were in America, four or five benefactors would already be providing me with a million dollars to try to bring new learning to this vital aspect of life that would help us all get in touch with our best humanity. In America, the Fetzer Institute says it –

> *"believes that the study of the mind's influence on the body –and of the relationship of the body, mind, and spirit – can provide the basis for developing precise and dependable approaches that will expand the scope of medical science and simultaneously give individuals greater control over their own health."*

I, in no way, diminish the significance of medical research, as we know it; of sociological and anthropological research as we know it. What I suggest and advocate is this additional research into soul health and the human spirit. What are the qualities that we need to release for our health and well-being?

1. Back in 1988, Dr C. Kuhn wrote on "A Spiritual Inventory of the Medically Ill Patient." He said, "Research to assess the relationship between spirituality and health is still in its infancy. Some factors which appear to be important in promoting optimal spiritual health and therefore physical well-being" include –

   - finding meaning and purpose in life-events

   - maintaining hope

   - participating in laughter and celebration

   - having an ability to love and forgive oneself and others.

Other scientists have said although the medical community may be hesitant to include spiritual concepts in daily medical practice, the majority of patients they treat believe that a spiritual approach to health care is vitally important. (*Advances* 1993, vol.9 no.4 p.70f)

Right at the core of our very being we all need to know there is a vital nurturing influence that changes and enriches our awareness of who we are, and that there is something good and worthwhile at the core of our being

Neenah Ellis was interviewing people in their senior years. She spent some time with Roy Stamper, aged 104. She said, "He is so charming", that it took her a while to realize that, despite his age (I would say just as much <u>because</u> of his age or <u>regardless</u> of his age), he still had "a fire inside him". That's a quality of the spirit – the core of being nurtured across the life span.

2.   I see some people and I think that their spirit has been locked up for years. But then I see them facing a task, a turning point, a trauma – and they are (like the fig tree) faced with a potentially transforming moment. Apparently from nowhere a layer of life breaks open and a stream of strength and compassion and kindness flows through. Sometimes we think our spiritual tank is empty and there is no forward thrust any more; and then the spirit tank opens, and we are likely to see a human being reaching out to their best humanity.

Judith Wright, in her poem Vision, wrote –

"He who once saw that world beyond the world –
so that each tree and building, stone and face
cracked open like a mask before a flame
and showed the tree, the stone, the face behind it –
walked forever with that beatification.
Waking at night, against the blank of darkness,

> *knew he contained it; touched hand upon brow*
> *and in his gladness cried, 'I, even I!'*
> *– knowing the human ends in the divine."*

The spiritual quality of transformation

3. I once experienced several winters in the far parts of the northern hemisphere. Some nights – cold and dark of the most eerie kind – a heavy black fog would roll in from the upper limits of the North Sea, bringing visibility virtually to zero. All through the nights and the next few days, as the fog lingered and refused to lift, foghorns sounded along the coast. Their forlorn and haunting warnings told every sailor out there on the wild seas that there were people on land caring and waiting for them. And they reminded people on land of people out there. Different worlds caring for each other, sounding through the dense fogs of life a sound of care and courage. Qualities of the human spirit – they make a vast difference to the way we live and cope.

4. We sometimes see that our fascination with all the gadgetry of life means we forget to react to the goodness of life. The spiritual qualities get suppressed. If we let them flow, the whole environment at a given time becomes softer,

more generous, and we touch our best humanity.

Health today is more than feeling okay physically. Health today is a combination of our physical health, our emotional contentment, our environment's qualities, and our psychological awareness. And then there is that spiritual quality that gives our physical existence its zap, its color, its anticipation; its special dimension of outgoing pleasure. Ultimately, the physical world only matters because the spirit comes alive and moves in it. What a huge loss it is, that we have been so eager to claim the physical and so slow to study the vital part of the spirit.

Robert Smith, professor of psychiatry at Michigan State University and director of the Centre for Meaning and Health, said it was most important that we distinguished mind from spirit. Speaking about only one aspect of the spirit, he said –

> *"Mind brings a person into a problem and helps them solve it. Spirit takes a person beyond the problem for a different kind of solution."*

Spirit becomes part of the process of meeting the problem and finding the solution.

5.   The qualities of the spirit become active in the environment. People become exuberant and generous. Dogs race up and down the mound. And we can all see the value of a flower or respond to the expansive pleasure of perfume.

I liked Grace Kelly's (Princess Grace of Monaco) words in her book – published before her death – My Book of Flowers –

> *"Flowers in every form and shape are one of the simplest ways of bringing life and colors into the home. There is a very easy way to prove this. Take an empty room with four white walls and ceiling. Place a plain container holding a bunch of flowers any-where you like in it. The eye immediately settles on this patch of color. The room is no longer empty. You can move the vase around to give different perspectives, but the effect is always the same. The room has life."* (p. 201)

5.   Here is the spiritual quality of creating life in an everyday environment.

4.   The spiritual quality: a process of meeting a problem and finding the different solution.

3.   The spiritual quality of giving out hope and courage.

2. The spiritual quality of bringing about a trans-
    forming moment.

1. The spiritual quality of nurturing the core of
    your inner being: keeping the inner core alive.

These qualities can't help but affect our life and as
we are able to release them and give expression to
them, they must contribute to the way we handle our
health problems, and the way we build our sense of a
life well lived.

THE HUMAN SPIRIT

Great Changes In Australian Spirituality

Des sat stirring his coffee until it was cold. He looked up and said, *"You know everyone expected me to go first. Nobody expected Rita to be the one to go. She was always busy. But then the cancer hit her and she was gone in six weeks! Nobody expected it. And nobody expected our oldest son to go at 46. A sudden heart attack; no one was with him. When they found him, he was gone. I had my by-pass six years ago. I'm not sure if it did me much good. I'm in a lot of pain – sometimes it's angina, sometimes it's my war injury, sometimes it's my wretched arthritis."*

I wake up every day, and I lie there wondering why. Why did I wake? Why should I get up out of bed? I keep thinking – I'm next. Part of me wishes that.

All my brothers have gone. I only have a sister left and she's no good. Her health went 10 years ago, but she's been a mental case for years.

My wife's sister kept dropping in to help me for a while after my wife died.

But when she saw I could be getting a bit sweet on her, she stopped coming, and I never see her now."

You can read further about Des in *The Doctor's Casebook - Discovering Wisdom and Contentment.*

At the end of chapter 26, I wrote –

"While Des almost resigns to a nihilistic future we might help him recognize that in his vulnerability and helplessness he may discover a larger self, a stronger self, and a nurtured and nurturing self." (p.235)

Des was a shrivelled-up individual – shrivelled up in health, enjoyment, expectation, authenticity and hope. He would not take us seriously if we said to him, "You are suffering from a deadness in your soul; a sickness of your inner spirit."

We have divided the health of the body from the healing of the spirit. We have split off the external signs of well-being from the inner sense of being alive. We have drawn a line to separate what he should do – do this, try that – from how he might discover a different way to BE.

Des is suffering from pathology of the spirit, and nobody comes to cure it. He, like many, will die of a diseased, underdeveloped, and demoralized spirit. Of course, we can pump him up a bit with some anti-depressants, and he will be able to "do" a few things more than he was doing – but what of the healing of his spirit? In the world of physical health, we may talk of an enlarged prostate, a swollen gland, of a distended vessel. In the world of the spirit we may speak of a contraction, a wasting away, a deficiency, a deadening of the spirit.

Is it important? Does it make any difference? Will we wait for a crisis? Is it like physical health to be monitored and proactively sustained? Will we have a full sense of being a person? Will our culture be any better? Will people be more authentic, genuine and generous?

The Resistance to Spirituality

There is a strong resistance to talking about the human spirit and especially about healing of the spirit.

1. It sounds too much like religion and church. With that there is an avoidance of the pietistic pressure to talk religious talk, to impose God onto a situation, or a supernatural intervention. It smacks of priests, preachers and popes all wanting to push their line and force a belief system on to the person.

2. It is mumbo jumbo land. We are fully committed to a scientific view of life and the healing process. What is more, the doctors' pills and prescriptions bring relief, while the religious view has been proven to be ineffective and irrelevant, and more than a little bit ridiculous – and religious people can be so phoney.

3. Spirit talk is so airy-fairy – it seems to say the real world of grief and suffering is somehow our fault – things of the earth and the body are bad, and we have made things that way. We are made to feel guilty about love and passion, sexual pleasure, money and wealth, enjoyment and fun. So we avoid talk of the spirit.

Rediscovery of Spirit

For decades many people have been speaking of a rediscovery of our spirituality. Long before the "new age" people were hailing its possibilities, the psychoanalysts and the humanistic psychologists were talking about it. For more than half a century, the existentialists have been talking about the rebirth of the human spirit.

In recent times many of the intellectuals have taken it on as something to be talked about in literature, poetry, and art. And we are expected then to read the writings of Patrick White and find in his damaged soul something of the rebirth of Australian spirituality. Or perhaps we are meant to stand back in front of, "Blue Poles" and see there – as I have never been able to – something of the profound moving of the spirit of Australia. Give me rather Lloyd Rees. Give me rather, Jill Kerr Conway's, *The Road from Coorain*, Alex Miller's book, *The Sitters* or Raimond Gaita's book, *Romulus My Father*, a discovery of Australian spirituality – all from the last decade.

And a very notable further example is Ruth Cracknell's, *Journey from Venice.*" It is pertinent that I never did warm to Ruth Cracknell in what I thought was a dreadful television soapie – called, I think, "Mother and Son". So it was with considerable resistance that I bothered to open up the cover of her book that described the paths of human anguish in the dying days of Eric, her husband. It became for her a wholly transformative experience in more than an ordinary way.

She described what she called a Venice where you "battle with the difficulties of the city on a daily basis". (p.256)

> "Yet, Venice gave me something else, something price-less that I cannot disown nor will I ever now be without. Lodged within my soul are the miracles of Venice. I do not know how else to describe the highly unlikely, the against-all-odds events that happened there. The Serene City that keeps the secret of her serenity, perhaps, solely for those in deep need – and who will only be able to recognize it much later, in recollection." (p.257)

And then at the end of the book she spoke of Eric and his last hours.

> "The closer he got to the end, the closer he seemed to be to this essence. In the grace of his dying, what I was looking at in the purest and simplest form was, I believe, goodness of spirit – and most miraculous of all – the interconnectedness of this spirit."

Descriptions of Spirituality

It is so easy to get into empty rhetoric and unhelpful generalizations as we talk about spirituality and Australian spirituality That is why I started with one man, Des. That is why I have spoken of Ruth Cracknell. One with no interest in the spiritual side of life even though he was in need; the other finding the spiritual side of life breaking in on her when she was not looking for it, and finding she was ready to reflect on it and respond to it.

There are five descriptions of our spirituality:

- It is a transformation of our consciousness: we are enlarged and connected in ways we were not before. Tolstoy called this his "consciousness of Life" that literally kept him alive

- It is a transformation of anxiety into a quietened contentment and grace

- It is a transformation of the emptiness and deadness in life into a responsiveness and authenticity

- It is a transformation of hostility and meaninglessness into a world-view of humanitarian wisdom and intelligence (See my book *Work*, chapter 13)

- It is a transformation of both life and attitude by a rediscovery of the resources of a liberating religion.

Australian Spirituality

David Tacey, in his book, *Re-enchantment – The New Australian Spirituality*, highlights the major ingredients of our spirituality. I was struck by the pathways that frequently seemed to run through his views –

1. Australians have two sides to them – the shallow, superficial side and the strength of their depth.

2. The white population, ignorant of what spirituality means, and uncertain about the black indigenous, different spirituality.

3. A secular spirituality and a wrestling with Australian religiosity, religious fanaticism and religious ignorance.

4. The "old" Australians and their ambivalence to multiculturalism.

5. A western or anglo-saxon morality trying to cope with the ethics and sexuality of a new age - the post modern age, the post 18th, 19th century church age.

6. Australian men trying to be nice to women, provoked by the feminine challenge to behavior, theology and morality.

7. The astonishing Australian landscapes, the earth, the ecology of the planet, and the eco-logical survival over and against an insatiable consumerism.

8. The rights of human beings to determine the way they will live and die, over and against those who want to control people in life and death.

Changes in Australian Spirituality

1. **Religious-less, God-less spirituality**
   People will discover their spirituality not out of traditional religions but out of the ques-tions and anguish of their experience. Des and Ruth! We will have a spirituality without relig-ion, a spirituality without God, or the God that the churches have been talking about – the medieval God.

2. **Readiness to be confronted with deeper things**
   We will have a spirituality of astonishing con-frontation with deeper things. Over my time at St Michael's, I have encouraged this. Way back we did an extensive internal refurbishing, probably more extensive than any heart-trans-plant operation to a human being. We opened

up the inside of this church and placed symbols here that had never been here before.

We installed rocks out on the corner with a mythical message to the city. We installed these magnificent stained-glass windows. We put Mingary, a sanctuary, in place. We have recited poems and conducted programs that speak to our psyche and our soul, our spirit and our culture's spirituality.

Why do we need it? We need to see that human spirits lose their energy, their hope, their life, and they fall into despondency, disturbance and depression.

We need to see that people can get so over-whelmed by their guilt that they no longer believe in their goodness.

We need to realize that the stress and noise of all around us can drive us into exhaustion and anxiety. So our challenge is the sacredness of silence – an energized silence that brings strength to the human spirit.

3. **A spirituality opened up by psychology and emotional growth**

The changes of the Australian spirituality will be seen in people's psychological insights, their emotional growth and their human relationships fulfilment. Our spirituality is not something restricted to the inner person but is a responsiveness to life and our whole social context. We cross the borders and the boundaries to find out what the human being can become. So we asked a German artist to do our windows, a Japanese sculptor to do our Mingary, and an Aboriginal woman to present us with the reconciliation flag.

It is about being spiritually alive without the suppression and restrictions of negative or restrictive religion.

- It is about confronting the deeper things

- It is about growth out of ourselves to others

- A spirituality where we see the good human being reaching out to living with both arms...

4. Spirituality will be a way of getting up from our previous uncertainty – and, as Jesus exhorted the man to do – walk into a different era, be different, better, more authentic and freer in life than we were before.

Morris West, whom I interviewed at St Michael's a few years before he died, said –

"It takes so much to be a full human being that there are very few who have the enlightenment and the courage to pay the price ... One has to ... reach out to the risk of living with both arms. One has to embrace the world like a lover. One has to accept pain as a condition of existence. One has to court doubt and darkness as the cost of knowing. One needs a will stubborn in conflict, but apt always to total acceptance of every consequence of living and dying." (Shoes of the Fisherman p.254)

5. **Spirituality is about restoration of many pathways**

   It is about reaching out to something beyond us that will restore those things we so quickly lose:

   - Our peace of mind
   - Our courage and purpose
   - Our union with the soul of the universe.

The Mingary prayer says it. It is about our spirits searching for that spirituality of a life enhancing restoration. The words are these –

Restore in us
A peaceful mind
A strengthened spirit

Restore to us
A new pathway
A new hope,
and a new purpose

Restore for us
The courage to
let go what is past
The readiness and
strength to walk
towards the future

Restore in us
A union with the energy
Of this sacred place
And a union with the
soul of the universe.

THE HUMAN SPIRIT

Courage to Talk
About Religion

In A More Honest Way

When I was a student and should have been focused on the designated subjects, I became intrigued by the distortions and skewed faces of Picasso's paintings. What was he telling me about life and our world, or was he just doing his best to see how screwed up he could make a painting look? I think he was saying – "You have one view of reality but Picasso has another." Which was more accurate, more honest?

Back in the 50s, Samuel Beckett wrote his play, *Waiting for Godot*. I read it with tenacious fascination. Here we were as immature, divinity students talking about something we knew nothing about, and here was Beckett saying – "Look at this, two old hobos waiting for God and they miss him." Perhaps we have missed him too. For the sake of honesty!

Then I read a little bit of Dostoyevsky's *Crime and Punishment* and *The Brothers Karamazov*. Ivan said to Alyosha –

> *"If the suffering of children go to make up the sum of sufferings which is necessary for the purchase of truth, then I say beforehand that the entire truth is not worth such a price ... We cannot afford to pay ... and therefore I hasten to return my ticket ... This I am doing. It is not God that I do not accept, Alyosha. I merely most regretfully return him 'the ticket'. "*

Trying to be honest.

Quite early on, I opened Jean-Paul Sartre's book, *The Age of Reason*, and I read –

> *"Man is alone, abandoned on earth in the midst of his infinite responsibilities, without help, with no other aim than the one he sets himself, with no other destiny than the one he forges for himself on earth."*

And just as I graduated and was striving to relate my little bit of theology to my little bit of psycho-analysis, in Oxford I came across an Anglican minister, R. E. Lee, also a trained psychoanalyst, and he said –

"There is a need for clearing away the rubbish that clings to Christianity so that it can be free to grow to its fullest strength and maturity."

I recognised a sharp fork in the road right there – either I must abandon this religious search, or I must clear away the rubbish and let a different religion grow to its fullest strength and maturity. For honesty's sake!

I have noticed that many people from within the churches have wanted to ensure that I was totally sidelined. And I have noted many people who have no adherence to any church who are too ready to describe me as rebellious – a renegade. All I would like is to have some honesty in our religious quest.

What I have been trying to do is to talk about religion in a more honest way. Thus, it was of intense interest to have Dr Robert Funk as our guest. He approached the whole matter from a different angle, different pathway and different scholarship, and yet we are both trying to talk about religion in a more honest way.

What kind of religion do we see? Too often, he said, it is a pompous religion that is not courageous enough to stay away from the rubbish and tell the truth. Too often we have the irish protestants beating their prot-estant drums, ready to kill their catholic neighbors. We have Fijians with guns held to people's heads and at the same time singing religious-drivelling hymns. We have a pope and many of his not-so-celibate priests opposing contraception, and there are millions of children affected by the AIDS virus, or otherwise starving in their poverty.

In Psalm 139 the writer is in awe of the God of the great mystery of life. What kind of God have we embraced?

Many people say the God we embrace is the God revealed to us in the bible. Well, I know my Old Testament very well, and I think it is a marvellous collection of stories and poetry, myth and legend. But there are also tales of "treachery and betrayal, incest and killings on a massive scale".

As Ludovic Kennedy wrote – some of the atrocities stick in the mind longer than others: Moses speaking with the voice of God telling the people of Israel to slaughter the Midianites –

> *"Kill every male among the little ones, and kill every woman who has known a man by lying with him. But all the women that have not known a man by lying with him, keep alive for ourselves."*

Joshua and the people of Israel killed 12,000 people of Ai, and the King of Ai was strung up and left hanging in a tree till nightfall. Elijah witnessed the triumph of his god over Baal, the god of storms, and then ordered that the 450 priests of Baal should be bled to death, and not one escape. And then do you remember Jael, the wife of Heber? She drove a tent peg through the forehead of Sisera while he slept.

It is one thing to ponder these brutalities. It is another to wonder about their relevance to religion today. Why do we go on saying the *"bible tells me so"*, when the bible has so many horrifying accounts, inaccurate stories, and so many inconsistencies. And to say we should embrace it as the whole truth of God and follow it word for word, makes nonsense of <u>it</u>, and makes <u>us</u> look ridiculous!

In my theological training, we had to sit through several boring lectures on the proofs of the existence of God. Unbelievable! If there were such unassailable proofs, why do so many people remain unconvinced?

You can't prove God exists. In any case there are always the two prior questions, "What do we mean by God? What kind of God?"

If you insist that God is a God who instills guilt and shame in a way no parent ought to ever do, then I'm not going to believe in that God.

If you insist that God is a God who prescribes a moral code for us in the same form as was accepted by a nomadic desert tribe 3000 years ago, then I find that incredible.

II

To have an honest religion, we have to examine the beliefs of this religion. Many of the doctrines still held by mainstream churches, and even more vigorously by the fundamentalist churches, are unbelievable.

It is said in the Old Testament book of Isaiah that a virgin would conceive and bear a son. The christian church took that over and built it into the virgin Mary legend. The truth is the word translated from the Old Testament as "virgin" was actually "a young woman". The virgin birth is sheer hoax. And as for her sexual virginity, do you remember the reading from the New Testament that shows Mary had at least six children; that sometimes she was deeply caring about her son Jesus or Joshua; and sometimes she thought he was mad.

There is the doctrine of the, "kingdom of heaven". Where is heaven? What does this phrase mean? Robert Funk uses the term, "domain of God". Years ago, I spoke of the divine economy. That did not seem to make it any clearer, so today I speak of the new way of being. The word Christ was a symbol of what Paul

Tillich called the new being. In Jesus of Nazareth we get a few glimpses of the new being and the new way of being to which Jesus continually pointed us in the here and now. And he called that the kingdom of heaven.

III

We have known, particularly over the past five decades and more, that much of the New Testament needed interpretation, revision, deletion and reconstruction. St Paul's view on women has long been regarded as unacceptable to us. His directions about food, sin and guilt have been largely rejected. We get very confused about his teaching on immortality and his longing to be with his Lord.

Robert Funk is a New Testament professor and scholar of 40 years, and his colleagues have been examining the texts to see which are authentic and which were myth and legend – all in the interests of a more honest religion.

IV

My pathway has been different, though it is not in conflict with the textual approach of Dr Funk.

I listened to Picasso and Beckett and Sartre and Dostoyevsky, because I could hear them speaking from the very depths of human anguish and searching. Do the teachings of the bible have anything to say to this anguish?

I absorbed myself in psychoanalysis, because there I could hear people exploring human pain and human possibilities. What does the biblical faith say to human pain and human possibilities?

I embraced existentialism because there I could hear scholars, and poets, artists and philosophers, asking the questions of human existence, facing despair, striving to find the courage-to-be, in spite of everything.

I found the theologian, Paul Tillich, drawing from the deep wells of faith and religion and from the distillation of the biblical texts and the bible stories, something of profound practical value to life and hope. From his writings I focused on several themes that transform the way religion can be integrated into life. This thematic approach is vital to an honest religion.

I shall today mention six themes. Sitting behind these six themes is a human need. The search for the historical Jesus is not so relevant unless we are searching for something. The people in the New Testament would not have listened to the sermon on the mount unless they had a need.

So we start from the human experience – the primary search: not, I emphasize, to be saved from our sins or to find our way to "heaven" or to escape the wrath of God. The search is for hope and healing, for meaning and purpose, for sense and transcendence, for the enrichment of life; for the wider exploration of health and wholeness.

The six themes –

1. God is a presence that always changes our perspective and our management of every stress and crisis.

2. This God-presence tells us we can BE HERE – we are accepted. We do not have to grovel in sinfulness and guilt, inadequacy and fear.

   We are accepted in spite of everything. And that acceptance is personal and political. It speaks to our inner need; it challenges every social and political discrimination.

3. We can get on quite well without God. We are given many resources. Just before the 1939 war ended, Dietrich Bonhoffer, a German theologian opposed to the Nazi regime, was executed.

He wrote letters from prison that have been quoted in these ensuing decades.

One letter said –

> *"...for the last hundred years or so ... it is becoming evident that everybody gets along without 'God'... As in the scientific field, so in human affairs generally, what we call 'God' is being more and more edged out of life, losing more and more ground."*

Many want to object strenuously and say we must work harder to keep God in people's lives. Perhaps God would like us all to grow up, be more honest, and use our religion in a different way.

4. Religion can lift us into a new way of being. Remember the "Kingdom of Heaven" concept was (is) about anticipation, excitement, embracing the possible. A new way of being – finding the pearl, the mustard seed, the harvest. There is expectation/enjoyment; there is an optimism/openness; there is an invitation/acceptance. It is all-inclusive, all-possible, all-searching for growth and generosity.

5. And there is courage. Through and through the stories of the New Testament and the Old Testament, there is the theme of courage. Again and again we are able to see through the

poetry, through the story telling, and through the miracle myths, and we hear the word: courage. We all need that courage to walk through the storms of our life. We all need courage to see new possibilities as we walk our Emmaus Roads. We all need courage as we find ourselves in a wilderness place and time, when we are wondering which direction to take, and what to do to be the people we are able to be, or perhaps meant to be. Bishop Spong said, "Our task is not to convert; our task is to call people into the depths of their own capacity to be."

6. In the Old Testament psalm we hear about the sense of wonder, mystery and faith. Professor and Principal D.S. Cairns, father of David Cairns whose name is part of Cairnmillar, once wrote this story of a young student who sacrificed his life in saving a boy from drowning –

> *"I want you to realise that scene. You have the whole nature cosmos around you there in symbol, sky and sea and hill and shore, and in the middle of it you have got this deliberate laying of life down. As you look at it you see this is no unconnected picture. Somehow it is all one whole ... I believe that somehow Nature was there in order that the man might do this thing; that in actions of this kind and the personalities that lie behind them, lies the clue to the riddle of the world, and*

> *the manifestation at once of the source from which that world came, and the end towards which it is working."* (David Cairns, S.C.M., 1950)

Every now and then, surely in the fullness of our honesty, we can pause to celebrate the mystery and the faith that keeps our searching alive.

1. The presence.

2. Acceptance.

3. Given resources.

4. A new way of being.

5. Courage to be.

6. A sense of wonder.

Conventional Religion! Who Needs It?

Five Breakthroughs To A Different Faith

People of conventional religion would like every-one to believe that they hold the high ground. They don't; in fact, huge erosion is taking place.

There are others who continue to belong in the wider circle of religion but they see their religion essentially as humanitarian and therapeutic.

The scuffle between the two is critically important to people throughout society – to those of religion and of none.

Conventional (christian) religion is hard to define, but like many makes of porridge – we all know it when we taste it. Here are five characteristics of conventional religion.

1. It assumes a divine right to impose its views of right and wrong on everybody. If that means dehumanizing some and destroying others, what of it? People have to be pulled into line. Gambling, euthanasia, sexual behavior, birth control, marriage, the role of women, the control of children – all come under a religious righteousness. Not long ago, it was dancing, card games, hotel trading hours, times when shops and cinemas could be open.

   Alongside these, little or nothing was said about the appalling conditions of the mental hospitals and jails, discrimination against women, and the hidden violence, abuse and suffering in homes and schools, and institutions.

2. Conventional religion is authoritarian, judgmental and punitive. It promulgates the view that everyone is somehow affected by the so-called original sin of Adam and Eve! And that people are therefore inherently bad. This religious talk of the sins from which everyone needs

to be saved deals in guilt and shame and instills fear to gain submission.

3. Conventional religion knows what God wants. It talks of the will of God as if God had made it known to them. It conveniently forgets what people of earlier centuries did in the name of God, to do his will. It speaks about the way of Christ without the slightest acknowledgment that we live in a world far removed from both the Old Testament commandments and the very fragmented glimpses we have of Jesus of Nazareth in the New Testament. The world we know of nuclear power, globalization, the rise and fall of stock markets, the internet and the medical and moral dilemma of when to switch off the respirator, was totally unknown when the pages of the bible were sewn together. Conventional religion is in a state of religious retardation while still believing it is speaking to a listening world.

Conventional (christian) religion has spoken of "upholding christian values", without any acknowledgment that people of other religions or none hold the same values. Or there may be that further assertion of christian values – especially on matters of sexuality and civil obedience – when Christ made no reliable or relevant statement on these matters. When and how do values become "christian" values?

4. Conventional religion speaks in a language that ordinary people cannot understand. It is part of the christian church's mystification. It adopts translations of the bible that are incomprehensible. It asserts the infallibility of the scriptures and continues to read passages that are anti-semitic, dehumanizing of women; as well as passages that are contradictory and unbelievable and often opposed to pleasure and enjoyment. People go in and out of church without understanding what it was about, and rarely protesting that what they heard was intolerable, or irrelevant and boring.

5. Conventional religion likes to believe it is politically significant. Its leaders like to be seen hob-nobbing with political leaders, particularly near elections. Politicians keep an eye on the conventional churches, not because they have great numbers who will do their bidding, but because they are likely to make a lot of noise. Politicians know that religion has always had a concealed layer of hypocrisy that can be manipulated and managed – and for votes that is what they aim to do.

Conventional religion has gone a long way from the young Jew called Jesus, or Joshua, who started it all.

Ask yourself these five questions:

1. Did he impose his views on people, dehumanizing some in the process, or did he encourage people to find their own strength and personhood?

2. Was he authoritarian, judgmental and punitive or was he one who reached out to accept people no matter who they were?

3. Did he lay it down that he knew the way to God's will, or was he a person of dialogue, pointing to the glimpses he had of what he thought the new being and new humanity would be like?

4. Did he talk in a language and a liturgy that few people could understand or did he tell stories that spoke right to their problems and pains?

5. Was he there to protect his turf or to help people see the possibility of new hope and a different world?

Those who are on the side of conventional religion are inclined to cheer when one stands firm to defend their declining cause. They are hailed as defenders of the faith. Whose faith?

The young Jew, Jesus, had no thought that years later his views would be converted into an institutional religion. In contemporary language, his words and his presence were therapeutic to those who came to him. He was pointing to a God who was generously accepting and to a humanity that could be compassionate, searching for life in all its fullness.

Though conventional religion still has its stalwarts, its conservative leaders, its hostile and vindictive preachers, their cause is lost. The game is up!

But the wider circle of religion – a religion that is therapeutic, humanitarian and life-enhancing – will continue to make a significant contribution to human society across all religions and cultures. We have seen five important breakthroughs during the past 50 years, and these breakthroughs have the potential to transform the ways in which religion will be embraced and applied to life in the future:

1. As we broke with fear and ignorance, we began to apply to our religion the high intelligence we have in other areas of life. With a liberated intelligence, we have begun to discriminate between what is believable and what is unbelievable. That is a major breakthrough!

We see that large sections of the bible display examples of shocking massacres, looting, raping and debauchery. There is the unbelievable violence of fathers to their daughters, of men to women and children. To suggest that these writings and these actions are inspired by God, or even directed by God, is unbelievable. To suggest that God would destroy this lot with a flood and save a few in the ark and then demand that this is history or literal truth, is to stretch ordinary intelligence too far.

Back in 1950, the then pope decreed that the mother of Jesus had been bodily carried into heaven, her virginity intact despite having given birth to Jesus, as well as his four brothers and two sisters. Unbelievable! How is it that the churches continue to appear ignorant of the mistranslation in the book of Isaiah, that "virgin" was the word used instead of "a young woman"?

But another pope came on the scene, Angelo Roncalli. At the age of 77, and on the twelfth ballot, was elected Pope John XXIII. He said, "Everyone was convinced that I would be a provisional and transitional pope. Yet here I am already on the fourth year of my pontificate, with an immense program of work in front of me to be carried out before the eyes of the whole world, which is watching and waiting."

He challenged unquestioned assumptions, launched new initiatives, set Vatican Council II on its way, and brought a revolution to the church's presence in the world. (*Leading Minds*, p.166.)

Many of the doors he began to open have been slammed closed. The lines have been drawn once again. But a continuing intelligent searching will examine what is believable and what is unbelievable?

I am astonished that there are numerous grown men today – in catholic and protestant churches – who still claim some right to tell people what they must believe. The freedom that we have to find our own ways to spiritual truth is now widely taken for granted. It was only after 1955 when Dr Margaret Knight of the University of Aberdeen made her two talks on the BBC, that people in Britain began to think outside their unchallenged narrow belief systems. In earlier years, people were incarcerated or executed for holding views that questioned the church's imposed position. On 8 January 1697, 20 year-old university student Thomas Aikenhead was hanged in Edinburgh, and the Reverend Alexander Findlater, who was at the execution, said God was glorified by this exemplary punishment.

Our freedom to exercise our intelligence has come slowly and sometimes at great cost!

2. The second breakthrough came with the German theologian, Paul Tillich, who had taken up professorial positions in America. He wrote the little book called *The Courage To Be*, in which his analysis of anxiety became widely read by existentialists and psychoanalysts alike. But it was his sermon on "You are accepted" that was the breakthrough. It proclaimed the most basic attitude and teaching of Jesus of Nazareth – a new conception of all-inclusiveness.

Jew and gentile, white, black and colored, this and that – all accepted. It was the forerunner to a wider inclusiveness that tests us today – Asian and African, heterosexual and homosexual, Hindu and Moslem, Shinto and Buddhist – accepted. (It was, after all, inconceivable that when Jesus fed the multitudes he would have said, "Some people here are going to go hungry, and they will go hungry because they are black or gay, or mentally disturbed"!)

Such acceptance means that the old image of God, excluding some and accepting others, had to go. Bishop John Robinson wrote an article in the London *Observer*, entitled "Our Image of God Must Go." Thereafter he wrote *Honest to God*, a book read by more non-christians than christians. There were others before John Robinson, like Rudolf Bultmann, and many others after, like Bishop Spong, Robert Funk and the scholars of the Jesus seminar.

3. For the third breakthrough, turn to Viktor Frankl or Elie Wiesel. They showed it was possible to emerge from the depravity and horror of the concentration camps and still believe it was worth searching for meaning in chaos, still worth searching for a sign of God, even though he was nowhere to be found!

Then came Nelson Mandela who, after 27 years in prison on Robben Island, emerged and said, *"I always knew that deep down in every human heart, there was mercy and generosity."* (Long Walk to Freedom, p.615)

Bishop Tutu said of Mandela's 27 years in prison:

"Mr de Klerk had not met someone vindictive, hell-bent on paying back the whites with their own coin, seeking to give them liberal doses of their own medicine. He found a man regal in his dignity, overflowing with magnanimity and a

desire to dedicate himself to the reconciliation of those whom apartheid and the injustice and pain of racism had alienated from one another. Nelson Mandela did not emerge from prison spewing words of hatred and revenge. He amazed us all by his heroic embodiment of reconciliation and forgiveness." (No Future Without Forgiveness, p.39)

Somehow, in those long years in an isolated prison, he must have been searching for the deeper meaning of life and the mystery of God's strange humanity.

There is one more story that must give hope to our humanity. America, one of the few nations of western democracies to hold on to the death penalty, recently saw a glimmer of change. Illinois Governor, George Ryan, declared a stay on all executions because DNA testing had shown innocent people had been convicted! Legislators in Maryland and Oklahoma are pushing for a stay in their states and a similar effort is being made in Pennsylvania.

That is definitely a major breakthrough. After such obdurate resistance to change, there is the recognition that science has brought a new glimmer of hope and meaning to a very bleak situation often supported by staunch believers!

4. The fourth breakthrough has come through psychology and psychoanalysis. Religion has not had a friendly relationship with these disciplines – not least because of the father of psychoanalysis, Sigmund Freud. He called himself "a godless Jew", and set religion in his sights as an oppressive and regressive influence in human society and in people's lives. His re-telling of the myth of the rebellion of the sons against the father did not endear him to the christian church. It resented his intrusion and resisted the acceptance of his views. For all that, the world owes him this debt at least – he opened up a new understanding of the human mind, showed us the inner conflicts that blocked our growth and freedom, and pointed to the illusions and fears that held us captive. He also explored pathways whereby people could leave their infantile dependencies and develop insight and resources to cope with life's confusions. No wonder the churches have been so frightened of psychoanalysis!

The influence of psychology and psychoanalysis has permeated many professions. In contemporary literature there are positive discussions of the way psychology and religion can be helpful to each other. Back in 1935, the British psychoanalyst, Dr Ian Suttie wrote his excellent book, *Origins of Love and Hate.* In it, he referred to religion as a "psycho-social therapy".

Much later (1987), the British social psychologist, Dr Michael Argyle, wrote that the benefits of religion are clear: first, it gives a meaning and purpose to life; and second, it is a source of valuable friendship and social support.

We at St Michaels would add a third benefit – religion encourages a belief in life and growth. It engenders positive emotions of caring and compassion, of celebration and joy. It presents the possibility that people can be expanded by symbols of great therapeutic and healing significance, as well as experiences of vital inspiration and a broadened world-view.

Psychology and psychoanalysis have brought a very liberating understanding of how religion can be a worthwhile influence in the human community.

5. The fifth breakthrough has been the candid admission that if religion does not help people to live, it is no good.

Religion is discussing the discovery of the meaning of "life in all its fullness" in a different, more colorful multicultural society.

Religion can help people grow (not only inwards) but outwards in tolerance and generosity, in maturity and grace. It can help people grow in their capacity to search openly and freely those further dimensions of life and our ongoing evolution beyond where we are now.

Morris West wrote –

"The act of faith is not a leap from darkness into light. It is an affirmation that light exists beyond the darkness ... We cannot endure to live in a mad universe. We are compelled, for our own sanity, to make sense of it. Sooner or later we are forced either to blasphemy or to the pilgrim search for the source of light – the shrine where creative love resides." (A View From The Ridge, p.9)

There are many residues of conventional religion that hang on to our coat like cobwebs. There is something in us that tends to resist change even though we see the change as necessary and inevitable. But these five breakthroughs are vastly encouraging. Look at them:

1. An intelligent, ongoing search for what is believable

2. An inclusive acceptance of a religion that drops its conditions

3.   Discovering meaning and hope in dreadful situations

4.   The value of the psycho-social therapy at the heart of religion

5.   A helpful, life-enriching religion; a religion that helps us cope with our stresses, consoles us in our failures and sorrows, encourages us to walk taller, and surrounds us with a network of stimulation and support

Search for this religion. We are searchers. There is a verse in the Old Testament book of Chronicles that says, "They searched for him – for he was hidden – and he let himself be found."

THE HUMAN SPIRIT

When a Stone is Rolled From Your Mind

Life Is Different: Religion More Healthy

C hristianity is dying. Those within the christian church deny the obvious reality. Churches are empty. Increasing numbers of people in so-called christian countries are vastly alienated from christian theology and church practice. Young and old alike find more in buddhist reflection and various meditations than they have ever found in the programs of the church. The islamic religion is now commanding more interest in the local marketplace than christianity has been able to sustain.

At St Michael's we chose not to march with the other churches on Good Friday. Why, you wonder? I'll tell you: because that view of christianity is ludicrous and out of date. They are still trying to hold on to a fundamentalist christianity while not really acknowledging their fundamentalism.

It is worth noting that St Michael's had more people here in the church on Good Friday than several churches in the city could put together for their march. And let us be clear: it is not a matter of the churches being united. There is no unity: scratch the surface and we are as far apart as the uniting church and the catholic church are divided on sexuality, on contraceptives, on the role of women and many other major concerns in modern society.

The cameras focused on a 9-year-old girl, and they asked what did Good Friday mean and she said, it meant, "Jesus died for our sins". What could that possibly mean to a 9-year-old? What sense does it make to a 50-year-old or a 90-year-old?

If you have come to church to hear that a young Jewish fellow, just over 30, died for our sins – and came to life again after his execution – then you are not going to hear that!

Today, christians have to make up their mind – either we live in a post-modern world or we continue to hang on to an outdated, ludicrous theology. We have to decide: are we living post-Copernicus, post-Darwin, post-Freud, post Bowlby, post-Margaret Mead?

A.N. Wilson (1999), in *God's Funeral*, asked the question,

> *"Is our religion that which links us to the ultimate reality, or is it the final human fantasy, the most pathetic demonstration in a spiritually empty ... universe?"* (p.16)

We have to throw out a lot of baggage to which we want to cling.

Wilson: "When religion becomes unbelievable or untenable, intelligent and sensitive individuals will reject it." (p.17)

1. Outdated religion says Jesus came down from heaven, spent some time on earth and then went back up to heaven. Whatever view you may have of heaven, scientific exploration has established beyond doubt that it is not up there. Yet the churches keep on reciting the creeds – that say the unbelievable – Jesus "for us men (forget the women) and for our salvation came down from heaven". The idea of a three-tiered universe is dead. The stone needs to be rolled away so that we see a new kind of world.

2. We have the idea that God sent his son into the world, to be murdered. Now how can anyone worship a God who would do such a horrible thing? A human father who arranged for his son's murder would not be given much room to move. It upholds a view of God as the ruler of the universe, sitting up there on a throne, intervening, authoritatively, and punishing people for bad behavior. It hangs on to the view that we have to somehow please that terrible God, or we'll cop it. And even today, we hear people say when they cop something, "What did I do wrong? Why is God punishing me?" This view of the old God is dead.

3. Then how come Jesus got into the business of dying for OUR sins. That's a bit rough! Suppose he died as a result of people's behavior back then; but how can he die 2000 years ago for OUR sins in 2001?

   We sang the hymn on Friday. We sing it every Good Friday –

   He died that we might be forgiven
   He died to make us good
   That we might go at last to heaven
   Saved by his precious blood.

   O, yes, we can sing it, but it is outside the boundaries of our belief. Its words are out of step!

They're no longer applicable. It stretches normal intelligence. It is based on a ludicrous belief system – that Adam and Eve were the first parents. That has been proven to be poetic and not fact. And because of their SIN (eating an apple), they then sexually transmitted their sin through the generations and we have the St Augustine (approximately 400 AD) nonsense of original sin: that human beings by that deed are forever sinful and they need a savior to help them become accepted by God. So they bound the savior and shed his blood - and by his blood we are supposed to be forgiven.

Wouldn't it be interesting if, instead of following Augustine and seeing the story of Adam and Eve as a demonstration of human sin, we saw it as a marvellous piece of human inspiration as the bible wrote, "Their eyes were opened"? Opened to their sexuality – why say that was a SIN? Suppose we take a different view and say that their eyes were opened to a new reality the world was unfolding to them. A new way of understanding the world.

4. But the sexual business did not stop there – Jesus had to be pure: that means to be sexless. So the religion said he was born of a virgin – even she had to be the subject of an immaculate conception and taken up bodily into heaven.

The claim was that sex and the human body were disgusting: that women were to be feared whenever they could not be pure. And all this is denial of the relationships Jesus had with the several women friends in those years we know a little about.

5. So the churches have come to assume a strange power over people: asserting that they had the door to God, and they had the authority to impose their commandments and prohibitions, with eternal punishment awaiting those who disobeyed. It would be ludicrous if it were not so punitive, and if it did not impart huge distress and guilt on so many people. The guilt factor has been very powerful and frightening, even though we know we have long since moved away from the world-view that gave it such power.

6. The further difficulty is that we say the spirit of Jesus lives on. It is often difficult to discern – even at the centre of the christian churches. We still hold onto a view that says religion has the say on how morality should be observed. But we all know we can be moral without God, without the church and without bishops and popes. There are many who say that the moral confusion of our time is because there are no clear-cut moral standards. But in a very real

and multifaceted world, whose standards will be imposed? So we pray to the holy spirit for guidance. They will do that in Rome to select a new pope. The present pope has ensured he selected 90 per cent of the voting cardinals. We might do the same but let them not call it the guidance of the holy spirit.

But we are not living in a first century christian world. We are living in a world of chemistry and computers, a world of vast statistics, of domestic violence and child abuse. We are living in a world where the power of money and military might wipe cities and people off the earth.

We are living without yesterday's God. Wrote Bishop John Shelby Spong -

> An external, intervening God *"is quite simply dead today, and those definitions of human life that force us to dream of atoning acts, sacrifices and stories of divine intervention are nonsensical. So the vast majority of the traditional Christ language has become inoperable. Jesus, as the agent of God's divine rescue operation, is not a Jesus who will appeal to, or communicate with, the citizens of this century."* (Why Christianity Must Change or Die? p.98)

What then can be said for the Jesus of the New Testament, the Jesus of the Resurrection Faith?

I have been speaking of this now for just on 40 years. Even as a student, I protested the nonsense of Jesus dying for our sins and rising for our salvation.

These past couple of years, I have hosted some overseas theologians and scholars, and will do so again this year. I have been amused that so many here have said, "Oh that's very exciting. Let's hear more." So let me state my position again and hopefully you will say, "That's very exciting, Let's hear more!"

The resurrection of Jesus was really the disciples seeing in Jesus what God was like. Suddenly their eyes were opened. They knew they were looking at the very presence of God. And they were excited about it. The stone was rolled away.

Their eyes were opened. And their task was then to open the eyes of others. Not because of God dogma, but because they could see that human beings would be different, nurturing, encouraging, inspiring and affirming.

1. A young Jesus of just over 30 was clearly a man of the earth and a man teaching that the old God was dead. A new God was rising (stone rolled way) and the new God was not an inter-

ventionist God, punishing people for their sins. The new God was a God who accepted people and sought people to accept each other. It is easy to say, but more difficult to do. More difficult to give up your commitment to hostility and punishment and become a person of understanding and acceptance. When the stone is rolled away, we start to be free of prejudice

- of race and difference
- of disease and mental illness
- of sexuality and sexual preference
- of women and menstruation
- of children and their rights.

Bishop Holloway wrote –

> *"Christianity has had too much to do with men who spend a lot of time justifying the exclusion of women.*
>
> *"Women's spiritual needs are not best met by institutions that are essentially instruments of hierarchy and guilt."*

(Godless Morality p.59)

The resurrection faith is about a new God who accepts us, in spite of, and because of, who and what we are.

2. The Jesus of the resurrection faith shows us the way to be free of our deep-seated fears and our psychological hang-ups. We can roll the stone away – and we (like the women of the story) see there is NOTHING there! But we go on, and live an inspiring life.

    So unlike us. When we see there is nothing there and nothing for us, we get nasty, disillusioned, or depressed. The resurrection faith is a faith that goes on and becomes an inspirational life! The mind gets blocked. But roll the stone from your mind.

3. He showed a remarkable courage to be a human being in the best sense. So much so that they said he had a God consciousness about him. Although he said he was there to point to a new God, many saw that new God was in him, and he was giving that new God to all he touched. Even to the thief on the cross, he had the courage and strength to say a comforting word to him. It was life-enhancing and life-expanding courage to be the best.

4. Through the bible we need to discover afresh what the real Jesus said. For generations, people have argued that because the bible says this or that, the debate finishes there. Nothing more can be said.

But read the scriptures (Old and New Testament) intelligently and you see there are large sections that no one these days would sensibly accept as the inspired word of God. It is deeply culturally determined; St John's Gospel is strongly anti-Jewish, and so on.

So many things, but what are the vital life-liberating essentials. We move away from the negativity of being saved from our sins and move towards the positive view of reaching out to our best humanity. That is the essential core of Jesus teaching – a new person, a new humanity, a new order with the God of life and growth, and possibility in every human life and in every human society.

We have been so strongly part of a society and church that have emphasized individual sins without fully recognizing the systems that breed those sins or the systems that those sins actually serve.

People settle for the absolute solutions, clear-cut authority or regress to them, instead of persisting with the greatest challenge of all: searching for our fullest humanity and our best possibilities. Our exploration of the mystery the new God will open to us.

Listen today for the Jesus Faith

1. Its acceptance.

2. Its freedom and inspiration.

3. Its courage to be the best.

4. The new humanity of growth and continual exploration.

Post christian, post modern, after Jesus, after Copernicus, after Darwin, after Freud, after Bowlby, after Mead; and always searching for a new resurrection, a new understanding of God and a new way of being for the world.

We see many children who have already lost the spark of spontaneity and they are not yet five years' old.

People each day in their adult years and old age show how life has hurt them and there is soul deadness within. Across groups and nations there is a readiness for hostility and prejudice, for selfishness, and for proactive and passive aggression.

Wherever you can help a new humanity to emerge, you are part of the resurrection.

No argument, no credal statement, no dogma is necessary, just the full affirmation of yes, the courage to be the best. When it is so easy to roll the stone back into place so that you cannot see the new possibilities, roll the stone from your mind; life will be different and religion will be healthy.

Buzzing Around Like a Bumblebee

When I had not reached 13 years of age, my father's aunt – my great aunt – heard that I was showing a slight interest in books. She was a small wisp of a woman and deaf as a post. From her dust-laden book cupboard she took four books she thought I should read. They were quite difficult I remember, but as I look back, I can see how they all carried a common theme. One was a book on bees. Another was Charles Darwin's, *Origin of the Species*. The third was Weymouth's modern translation of the New Testament and the fourth book was about Freud's theory of the unconscious mind. Human beings are very much like a tree – you see what is above the ground, but the root structure is underground (and like the unconscious mind) it is of critical importance for what happens above the ground.

All four books were united in a common theme – what we see of the human being is only part of the mystery, part of the wisdom, part of the vast and exciting context in which we all live.

We have found many things to persuade us to shrug off the mystery. We have run into many experiences that question all given wisdom, and we have moved increasingly into the business of expanding and defending our individualism and we have lost our sense of living in a life-enriching context.

The book on bees attempted to describe the mystery of the spirit of the hive: the amazing sense of timing, of working for the hive, and knowing the moment to lift off and swarm as a hive to another place. While building their hive, each bee does its work but always comes back to the hive. The bee finds its life only in the context of the hive. Isolate it, and however abundant the food, or favorable the temperature, it will die in a few days – not of hunger or cold, but of misery, separation and loneliness. Apart from the hive, it loses its place and purpose, its direction and joy, and nothing will console it.

So you left the window open and in flew the bee. You will see this bee's frantic attempts to find its way out. About 18 months after I read this book on bees I was at a rural secondary school – and whatever prompted us to do the following I don't know – but two of us went to the local town hall to a CAE concert in which John Armadio was playing Rimsky Korsakov's "Flight of the Bumblebee".

I often think in our therapeutic work how often people are behaving like that bumblebee.

I ask the question, why are sacred times and sacred places back on the agenda? I have written a larger paper on this subject, with which I give eight reasons. Here are two of them:

1. We have lost our sense of who we really are, and for a large part of our lives we are stranded somehow behind our window panes. Some of us don't know what this phase of our life can possibly be, and some of us are buzzing up and down to the sounds of Korsakov's "Flight of the Bumble Bee".

2. We have lost our sense of being connected, living in context, in the spirit of the hive. So we buzz all over the place.

Actor, Peter Coyote wrote, "If you're always on the run there's no place to rest. You're continually taxing the power of your mind and imagination."

In the New Testament we read that Jesus took his disciples aside. They had been so busy and preoccupied, they had not had time to eat. So he said, "Come on, let us find a quiet place where we can rest awhile."

The human body can turn on itself. The mind can turn on itself. So can the human spirit. The organism starts to sabotage itself, undermine its confidence, and destroy its capacity to stay alive.

A Quiet Place

A quiet place helps restore harmony and health to body, mind and spirit. A quiet place gives you the time and the place to say, "Let me reaffirm what life is about."

Leo Tolstoy, out of his moods of melancholy and depression, cited the story of Anna Karenina. The story began with a moral man disillusioned with marriage, and ends with a moral man in a remarkably similar state. In between, there are two railway deaths and struggling attempts to make something of romance. But the greatness of this book is in its moments, scattered throughout, moments that are full of life, and affirmations of the belief in life.

We need sacred times and quiet places to restore what life is about and to reaffirm our belief in life, lest the subtle and even unconscious processes draw us into different forms of destructiveness.

Solace

Sacred places are important as they provide the possibility that we can reach beyond our ordinary places to find the comfort and solace we need.

Frank McCourt, in his book, *Angela's Ashes*, told how as a small boy, he found great solace as he talked to the angel on the seventh step. In those terrible conditions, enduring the worst parenting, in the midst of grief and anxiety over the death of one child and the birth of another, Frank McCourt, the small lad, made a sacred place out of the seventh step of the slum in which they lived.

Karlo Stajner wrote of his imprisonment in Joseph Stalin's gulags, *7000 Days in Siberia*. Out of excruciating pain, he and his fellow prisoners looked towards the end of the war with a mood of incredible optimism. "They all said the same thing, 'the war will be over soon and we're going to be released'." Stajner was less sanguine about their prospects but he wrote in his journal, "How good it is that no matter what befalls them, people never lose hope."

We need our sacred times and sacred places where some solace can be found from our different pains, and where some hope can break through the events we struggle to understand. We are seeing that our rituals around our sacred places may be "as important as mental health services for a community's health".

A Larger Place

The Gospel story told us that the crowds of people sensed they were connecting with something larger than themselves. They were being lifted to a larger view and translated into a larger context. We need our sacred places to lift us to a larger awareness of the world of the spirit.

John Shaw Neilson's poem of "The Orange Tree" was doing this –

> *"The young girl stood beside me I*
> *saw not what her young eyes could see*
>
> *There is a light, a step a call,*
> *This evening on the Orange Tree."*

Marjorie Pizer described this larger connection in her poems of healing –

"The sun reached out his hand to me
And touched my face
And so my healing began."

Des Pres described an incident in Auschwitz. In the dead of the night, an old man began to chant a prayer recited in the week proceeding Rosh Hashanah (a high holy day of the Jewish New Year). Wrote Des Pres –

> *"All life had ebbed out of them – all at once the oppressive silence was broken by the plaintive tones of the prayer.*
>
> *There, close to the wall, the moonlight caught the uplifted face of the old man who, in self-forgetful, pious absorption, was singing softly to himself ... His prayer brought the ghostly group of seemingly miserable human beings back to life... We sat up very quietly, so as not to disturb him. He did not notice we were listening, but when at last he was silent, there was exaltation among us. An exaltation which men can experience only when they have fallen as low as we had fallen, and then through the mystic power of a deathless prayer, have awakened once more to the working of the spirit. Our sacred times and sacred places lift us to a larger awareness; we are awakened to the working of the spirit."*

In 1999, the St Michael's community reconstructed a chapel into a sanctuary called, "Mingary – the quiet place". Mingary is a sacred place. It's where people can stand in their sadness and sorrow and find a sanctuary that lifts them from their earth-bound pain and longings to connect with the healing solace of the world of the spirit, this world of a new courage and a new way of being.

Best Possibilities

The gospel narrative showed how people could move from being like sheep without a shepherd to being people who celebrated the gifts of life.

We need our sacred times and sacred places to remind us of one of the great teachings of the faith – the importance of realizing who we are and what we can become; and how our environments can be enriched to help people achieve their best potential – the blessing of life fulfilled.

Amelia Barr, who back in 1908 wrote the book, Three Score and Ten, said –

> *"I wish to feel alive to the last moment, to preserve my vigor of mind and ready sympathy in all that happens."*

And H.W. Longfellow wrote –

"What then? Shall we sit idly down and say, 'The night hath come; is it no longer day?'

Something remains for us to do or dare;
Even the oldest tree some fruit may bare."

Our sacred times and sacred places call us out of all our tendencies of halted growth to achieve our best growth and best possibilities at whatever stage of life we are moving through.

Nelson Mandela, in his inaugural speech in 1994, said –

"Our deepest fear is not that we are inadequate. Our deepest fear is that we are powerful beyond measure. It is our light not our dark that most frightens us. We ask ourselves, who am I to be brilliant, gorgeous, talented and fabulous?

Actually who am I not to be? You are a child of God. Your playing small doesn't serve the world. There's nothing enlightened about shrinking so that others won't feel insecure around you.

We were born to make manifest the glory of God that is within us. It's not just in some of us. It's in everyone. As we let our light shine, we unconsciously give other people's permission to do the same. As we are liberated from our fear, our presence automatically liberates others."

We need our sacred times and sacred places –

1. To restore harmony and health to body, mind and spirit; to reaffirm our belief in life.

2. To find the comfort and solace we need.

3. To connect us with something larger than our-selves – the larger world of the spirit.

4. To lift us to celebrate the gifts of life, fulfilment and potential; to a better view of the world.

Rebuild Your Personality

After Times Of Damage

F ay Weldon in her book, *Rhode Island Blues*, told how Sophia Moore was affected by the long-ago suicide of her mother. Sophia had a recurring dream in which her mother jumped into the middle of the road with a sign that read, "Your fault, Felicity" (thus blaming her mother). On the other side it read, "You are to blame, Sophia" (blaming her daughter). The mother's death was bad enough, but the dream left a deeper, more disturbing and persisting anxiety.

You will have seen how many people can visit great and lasting damage on each other – by their behavior and accusations, and by fears and images they leave behind them.

A male pedophile can leave a lifetime of psychological damage on the innocent, developing personality of a child. The bully at school leaves not only a memory but also a residue of fear and resentment in those who were made to cower as inferior victims before the daily or unpredictable onslaughts. Parents can be so focused on their compelling objectives, their daily agendas, their self-assured dogmas and their highly protected principles, that they do not recognize the damage they have done to their children's personalities.

Personality damage affects enjoyment, general functioning and the way a person envisages and meets the future. The f's are all involved: how they feel, function, fantasize the future, bring focus to their self-worth and what level of fulfilment they find.

Personality damage is reflected in a persisting conviction of having been hurt by others or by the events of life. There is a loss of enjoyment, pleasurable participation and motivation. Distressing memories are repetitively irrigated, and there is a storage of negative moods and emotions, perhaps with only fragments of a belief that a full recovery is possible.

How then can we rebuild a damaged personality? Some psychologists contend that rebuilding is only possible through the mediation of complex psychological treatment. But we know that other resources of music and poetry, meditation, and inspiring and supportive relationships, can play a significant part. Some are exploring what existentialism and religion may bring to the processes of rebuilding.

There are several steps that can be taken to facilitate the rebuilding of personality after some damage:

1.   Constantly recognize and reduce the invasive action of the "damage". Act to prevent further damage. Avoid places and people that are likely to reactivate the damage and its memories, moods and emotions. Only go back to your damaged places and experiences when you are confident and strong enough to cope with all that it will entail; or go with people who can competently guide you through to that desired state of closure and completion.

2.   Reduce the negative emotions and increase the positive healing emotions. The negative emotions may deceptively entice you to believe in their validity and value, but keep examining whether they are part of the necessary pathway towards rebuilding and release. The negative emotions are persisting grief and psychological pain, and pathological sadness, guilt and shame, depression, self-blame, desolation and despair. The positive emotions are pleasure, anticipation, hope, enjoyment, laugh-

ter and the ebullient emotions of a life worth living.

It is common to find that people will readily claim that they have ample positive emotions, but frequently we find that when those emotions are most needed, they cannot be seen. In my youth I lived far into the country. One farmhouse was the custodian of the fire tank for a vast district. The tank was left up on a stand through the year. You could see it as you drove by. In the summer time, when a fire broke out, the farmer would reverse his worn-out truck under the stand, lower the tank on to it and off they would go to get water into the tank. After the long period when the tank was not used, it rusted. When it was most needed, it could not hold its water!

People can be like that: they give the appearance of readiness, but when their positive emotions are most needed, "the tank" has no water in it.

Recent studies on cardiac psychology have shown that people with heart disease were 40 per cent less likely to laugh in humorous situations than those with healthy hearts. You might say they had let their "laughing tank" run dry and rust. They not only laughed less;

they were less likely to recognize humorous situations.

3. You can intercept the flooding and reirrigation of distressing memories you know will upset you. This is both a private and public task. In your private moments, you will know how quickly you can slip into revisiting memories that evoke sadness and grief, guilt and anger, resentment and rage. In public you see it all too clearly at funerals, especially when people feel a need to expose and ventilate sensitive and distressing memories that evoke diffusely uncontrolled behavior. Those who come to offer comfort and support find themselves the uncomfortable observers of a grief that can find little relief in such public ways. It does not do anybody any good. Though some are ready to reassure the grief-stricken that expressions of grief are appropriate – even healing – care and sensitivity are necessary, lest the people most concerned find they have to cope with the memory of their catastrophe and the catastrophe of their public grieving.

You will know how easy it is to keep old wounds and grudges alive by revisiting and reirrigation. "It was what he said. Yes, it was 22 years ago. But I will never forgive him." Some war veterans keep alive their hatred for "the enemy". They turn that wartime hatred into life-long prejudice passed from one generation to another. They cannot accommodate the notion that war always brings out humans' primitive brutality and barbarity – on both sides. Those who suffered were the victims of people often far removed from the immediate zone of suffering. There is a sensitive balance between an appropriate remembering of those who were killed and injured, and the harboring of bitterness, and the vital need to be part of those processes that preserve peace among people who are ready to resort to violence and war to achieve their ends.

4. You can explore pathways of self-healing. When a house is blown down in a storm, people gather to rebuild it. So, when a personality is damaged, we need to look for the right restorative environment, resources and people so we can facilitate a rebuilding. You can become part of a self-healing process, taking time out; listening for voices that encourage you; setting aside places and symbols that keep you focused on the new reality in which you must continue to live.

Group therapy can be a valuable self-healing experience for people. Therapist and patient collaborate, and with others in the group, neutralize destructive tendencies and mobilize optimism and hope, helping each person become their own recognized agents of self-healing and change.

5. You need to change your status and your self-description constantly. When you have been damaged, you are likely to describe yourself in terms of your damage:

> *"I was bullied at school."*
>
> *"I was abused as a child."*
>
> *"I was a victim of the Pol Pot regime."*
>
> *"I had shocking parents."*
>
> *"I was nearly killed in the war, in the accident, in the fire."*

You can allow yourself to be known by your damaged part:

> *"I lost my child and you can never get over that."*
>
> *"I suffer from nightmares since the burglary six years ago."*

You can become a walking record machine. Just let someone switch you on – and out comes your story for the five thousandth time.

But then you met Lawrie. Fifty years after the war, his family discovered for the first time what he had endured. "You would never have guessed," people said. Lawrie quipped,

"I just got in with life. You can't live in the past. You've got to move forwards. Life is a once-only event; I saw it was too precious to say I was a victim. I'm never going to be anybody's victim. No matter what happens, you can turn it around."

Lawrie did not describe himself by what he was. Nor did he inhabit environments that reminded him of what he was. The past was one part of a multifaceted personality. The question is always, "What are you now?" People who had something in the past can be terrible bores in the present.

It is far from easy! If someone did you a dirty trick and deeply hurt you, your life may shrink. You become a shrunken personality – even though you may be harboring a lot of anger and frustration. You are no longer the personality you once were and could have been. Refocus then on your best status – forwards.

Stewart Conn, in his poem to his sick and dying friend, wrote –

*"Thanks to you we see
things differently, more acutely:*

love detectable, where
we never thought to look.

So –
Above all, may a miracle
yet happen:
a white, not a black sail
appear over the horizon."

You can constantly keep encouraging people to fly the white sail! That white sail says – "In spite of all we have been through, we are alive. Alive with some joy in ourselves, and some hope to bring to others."

THE HUMAN SPIRIT

Sometimes We See the Miracle

I first became conscious of cancer when I was in my middle teens. My mother developed an illness that had no name. In the best years, when she was about to enjoy the satisfactions of a competence and sense of purpose that had grown and flourished in the first five decades of her life, she quite suddenly became the victim of pain and a slow, relentless deterioration. The pain became beyond endurance for her and for those who watched: it also defied all analgesics and the increasing doses of morphine. Surgeons moved from one zone of her body to another like dogs trying to find rats in a haystack. They knew something was there but they did not know exactly where to look next. She moved through several hospitals – enduring surgery, convalescence, traction, inserting pins and plates, and always the sleepless, nauseous pain. A woman who was once vigorous, high-spirited, and a source of strength and enjoyment to many people, became, over seven years, a withered helpless body. But even in those last 18 months, she strongly resisted the approach of death that made three separate, violent visitations. In the last 18 months she had two massive hemorrhages. Her doctors on each occasion said it was only a matter of a day or two and she would be gone. But she recovered. As with Lazarus, it was as if there were more living to be done. It was hard to see why she survived those two attacks, before ultimately succumbing to the third insufferable devastation. There were four things:

1. She had long practised the art of inner reflection and meditation. Despite her busy life in a large family, she nurtured a patient contemplation of nature, an enjoyment of song and music, and she was unafraid to show she knew how to be alone in the silence of the world.

2. She had an optimism and strength of soul that at the time was incredible and, in retrospect, was inspiring.

    For Christmas 1952, a year before she died, I had the youthful audacity to give her Dr Arnold Hutschnecker's new book, *The Will to*

Live. In a book 40 years ahead of many of today's professionals, Hutschnecker talked of how the will to live is vital to health and recovery. He wrote, "To live long, not only in years but in the enjoyment of them, we must understand and control the forces which shorten life. Both early and late, we must take time to cultivate the will to live."

The book was saying then what years later would be confirmed and made respectable by medical and psychological research.

Peace and friendship grow from the same roots as health and happiness. As we strive for the one, we win the other. All are the flowers of a sturdy and vigorous will to live. "To hate is easier, but it is healthier to love," wrote Hutschnecker.

And that was woven into her attitude. I remember our minister saying the words of Robert Frost, "you only get to see the light from the stars when it gets dark".

3. She stayed alive because of her awareness of people gathered around her.

We talk today about support groups, caring cells, a healing aura. We did not talk like that then. We just were!

I have no doubt that the doctors and nurses were as vital as the family. We were all there. It convinced me then, that after all the interventions are completed, the environments we create become the vital zones of healing. By attitudes, thoughts, prayers, mood, words and our presence, we can create an environment for healing to take place, for courage to be renewed.

4. She stayed alive until those of us around her could hear what death was saying. Through our losses, new pathways open. Through our losses, we grow in a different way. Through our losses, the paint brushes of mystery and wisdom pass across our faces. I find that some people wait until those close to them are touched by the color of those brushes and then they are gone.

II

Since that personal encounter with cancer, I have sat with many people thus affected. Some were dying; others recovered. There are many extraordinary stories both of the dying and of the remarkable recoveries. I often ponder the various expressions of malignancy as I see them. There is the malignancy that hits for no apparent reason and we become the unwilling host of a disease. It is not easy to see why this has happened: but then it becomes the task to respond. There is the malignancy that comes our way because of our lifestyle, our destructive behavior and our health-risking habits. There are the stresses of life; the emotional traumas; the simmering anger and the frustrations we refuse to resolve. We carry loads of emotional barbed wire around inside us: to hell with all that talk about the will to live. It seems all we want to do is simmer and suffer, to hack and hurt each other. There is the malignancy that seems to characterize our world: the mental attitudes; the destructive modes of living; the chemicals that are accepted as daily food and the radiation in the atmosphere. It sometimes appears that we would prefer to poison the whole ecological system than live and let live.

III

What has been our approach to these three malignancies? In the western world we have been unconvinced that malignancy has anything to do with food, the air, our lifestyle, our attitudes or our moods. We have been symptom oriented. Pathology oriented. Treatment oriented. And we have been slow to recognize how our attitudes and lifestyles affect our health and well-being. I remember that, not long after I came to St Michael's, I spoke of how mood and stress affect the body-mind equilibrium making us vulnerable to diseases such as heart disease and cancer. One doctor was so irate; he told me to stick to the bible and leave the issues of health to the people who knew about them. I told him I would do just that. The people who know about them are the people who continue to search: we are all in that. He showed, in the way he left, that he did not want to be part of the search. Today, there is wide and growing acceptance that there are several ways to manage our malignancy. We in the west have placed a strong emphasis on the adversary approach. When you have a malignancy, we tend to bombard it, to try to beat it. In doing so, we may at times create an environment where our inner, ongoing healing is made more difficult. The psychological approach, using some strands of eastern philosophy, has emphasized:

1. The role of the patient in the healing alliance.

2. The mood and nature of the relationship that the doctor fosters with the patient is more a gentle alliance and partnership.

3. The creation of healing environments and of attitudes.

4. The talking "cure" of psychotherapy where the person gathers a different perspective on the

malignancy, the stresses in their life and their own resources.

5. The role of optimism, hope and faith in the healing process.

6. The inner environment, the inner mood, reflection, meditation and the waiting for a harmony, and searching for a union with the source of life.

IV

Our beliefs have changed –

- From the doctor cure to a partnership in process

- From the external interventions to creating inner healing environments

- From discounting hope and faith, to rediscovering the value of the will to live and the part of faith

- From much doing to the discovery of being.

The passage from the book of Revelation (22:1-5) places before us a picture, an image. Images can be so powerful in the process of healing and health. There are four images:

1.   The water of life. It comes as an agent of cleansing to our whole life, to the body, to the mind, to the spirit and the systems of the world. The water of life is the agent of refreshment, renewal and rejuvenation. It is a powerful image of your meditation.

2.   The tree of life – the image of nature, of food, of foliage, of beauty, of growth, of abundance. It is a symbol of God's caring, providing and ordering. And most importantly the tree emphasizes life, life, life ... The throne of God: in all our striving, what is of ultimate importance? Where is that which has some sovereignty, some central supremacy, which gives a core and substance to everything else? The image here is the Throne of God; that is where we do our worship. Listen to what Ian Gawler wrote –

> *"Everything becomes more important when our experience of life is viewed as a temporary privilege to be here, not an open-ended party. The minor hassles of life pale into their insignificance, major challenges are confronted and dealt with, the unfinished business in our lives becomes an urgent priority to resolve and the enthusiasm to transform bad habits into creative ones is strong indeed.*

Meditation aids this whole process. It, too, leads us into an experience of what is real, of our own real self. It provides the balance and equilibrium that gives the freedom to make changes in our lives and enjoy it to the full.

People who touch all this really do come to life through cancer. If you do not have cancer you could want to experience that 'something special'. Here are two recommendations. Firstly, establish a regular practice of meditation. Secondly, do this exercise:

Imagine a fantasy situation where your life is guaranteed to go on for the next three months. You will have all the same potentials, health and possibilities you have now but after those three months, your life will end with certainty. The exercise is to write down the 10 most important things that you want to do in those three months.

This is the challenge exercise. It could transform your life." (Newsletter, Spring Issue, 1986).

Life as we live it can be all over the place – or maybe there is a sense of discovery where we will do our worship: where we will find some centre and say, "Here is what really counts!"

They will have a name upon their foreheads. It says those who come close to the caring and healing presence carry the name on their foreheads. It is never removed. It is always there. In life. In pain. In dying. The name of the one who cares is still written on our foreheads. The whole christian story is one of great hope pervading human suffering. Jesus walked into the gaping anguish of suffering and said, "Little maiden arise", and to the gathered community he said, "Give her something to eat." At once, his name was on all their foreheads. They were part of the healing environment (Mark 5:41f). As he himself took suffering upon his mind and body, he could say, "In my father's house are many mansions," I go to prepare a place for you. His name is written forever on our foreheads. The water of life, the tree of life and the throne of God are all there as part of images of hope, health and life – images of our meditation and nurturing. But we look again to see if they really do have something personal to say to us. And then we remember. Do you forget? Let me remind you; his name is written on your foreheads. That is very personal!

Notes:

There is a conflict in most people's minds whether personality is a fixed and stable entity, or whether it is subject to change as we grow older, and as we are affected by situations and life events. Personality is a multi-factored expression of an individual's management of life generally and of any specific situations. Personality is made up of such factors as mood, behavior and attitudes, character and charisma, self-perception and self-portrayal, participation in relationships with others, and the conceptualization of the world. It is what gives a person a subjective experience of identity and assists in that changing process of his/her public identification. Several examples are given. In the latter part of the essay above, a story from the New Testament is used to illustrate several elements that are of central importance for the way the response to life-events is influenced and personality is changed. The story does not embrace all factors that lead to personality change, but those that are given form a basis for further extension of this applied approach.

THE HUMAN SPIRIT

Get Up There with the Ginger Cat

Each day I emerge from my door to take an early morning run or walk. No one in the neighborhood is ever out there to greet me. But I am regularly greeted by a ginger cat that actually lives up and around and in the next street. He has discovered where I come from, and I'm barely out the door, and he is rolling and writhing around my feet. He gives the impression of one with all the energy of having just emerged from a long night's sleep, but I suspect he has been out tomcatting all night. Well, off I go after a pleasant interchange of greetings and off he goes until the next time.

But one day he did not appear. An hour or so after my run, as I drove to work, I rounded the corner, and caught a glimpse of that ginger cat. He had scaled the fence in the neighborhood and there he sat gazing upwards into the tree as if considering whether he could make that flying monkey leap from fence line to foliage. I stopped, got out and went across to engage in conversation with this cat who, when rolling on the ground, showed he was happy to be my friend. But up on the fence, fully half a metre above me, he refused to recognize me or even lower his eyes to my level!

During the night some cat prophet called Habakkuk had told him that rolling around in the dirt was not the only place to be – that the God of all cats had given him feet to leap and walk in the high places. God, rich in goodness and generosity had given him a glimpse of a different way to live. The God of the cat is also the God of little children and he touches them all with curiosity and awe and spontaneous belief in great possibilities.

What a pity old cats and old, old cats just loll about. Like human beings, as they pull themselves along the life span, they begin to believe that the only way to live is to loll.

But here I saw this late middle-aged cat was giving me a message. It was saying on that day: if you want to talk to me, come up to my level. Climb up here beside me. Everything is different up here. I looked around and one or two people were now out walking – and well, there was no way I could get up on that fence to talk to the cat, so I retreated to the car. As I put the seat belt on, I glimpsed back. He was looking far beyond me with a superior mesmeric mind, indicating that he was seeing something I would never see. Everything is different up there!

Three passages of scripture have become great favorites. The little minor prophet Habakkuk knew he had been down in the pits for a long time. Life was not good. He had put in a lot of effort, but failure was all around him. Yet, he said, in spite of all that –

although the fruit trees will not blossom and the olive crops fail; although the sheep die off, and the cattle do not produce new calves – God keeps me believing that I can have hinds' feet and he helps me walk in the high places (Hab. 3:18-19).

The Epistle confirmed the belief: God rich in goodness and generosity has opened another way (Ephesians 2:1-7), and in the Gospel, Jesus said –

"Put no obstacles in the way. Let your heart be like the heart of a child – full of curiosity and awe, and expanding with energy and a spontaneous belief in great possibilities that are still in front of you."

Here, today, we have people at three points of the life span. We have baptized these tiny babies and blessed them with the possibilities of God's gift of a good life. We have people here who know this is senior citizens week, and some of you are over 90 years of age. And the third group is the rest of us – in between. Good sages make no distinction in ages. We are all one age – searching for sensible aging with growth and enchantment.

All of us can get up there with the ginger cat! You will be quick to point out that I did not pass the wall-climbing test. I did not get up there. But I often say to people, "imagine what it would be like". Climb up there in imagination. Climb up there in spirit. Climb up there with all your existential mobility. Climb up there with the energy of empowering transcendence. Climb up there as if the God of cats and creatures and all creation is opening to you a new way. "Everything is different up there."

Listen to what goes on in the cat:

1.   Up there the world looks different.

2.   Up there he feels he is different.

3.   Up there he is connected to a different longing.

4.   Up there he is connected with a different en-ergy.

Get up there with the ginger cat! What will that mean for all of us who are wanting to lay claim to a sensible aging; a successful aging; a sensible adulthood; a sensible autonomy; a sensible aspiration always with growth to the body and mind and expansiveness and enchantment to the soul?

1.   Put some emphasis on the rising of the bread, the rising of the sun, the rising of the spirit. Put emphasis on rising above the difficulty and demoralization.

Lord Byron, in 1817, tried to revisit in mind what it must have been like to be Torquats Tasso locked in prison in the 1560s. He called his poem "Lament of Tasso" for Tasso used his writing to rise above his dire situation:

> *"For I have battled with mine agony*
> *And made me wings where-with to overfly*
> *The narrow circus of my dungeon wall*
> *And freed the Holy Sepulchre from thrall."*

It was the 17th century philosopher Pascal who, knowing the despair of so many, would write

> *"Where the universe has crushed him, man can*
> *still be noble than that which kills him."*

In psychological circles we speak of an inherent need in all of us to create some myth or metaphor or meaning that helps us transcend our biological fragility. We yearn to create an adequate personal story that gives our passing years a sense of purpose and fulfilment.

We all are enhanced as we find a way to take hold of the realities of our sorrows and stresses, our foibles and failures, and in mind and spirit rise above them.

Wordsworth wrote –

"And I have felt
A presence that disturbs me with the joy
Of elevated thoughts; a sense sublime
Of something far more deeply interfused..."

2.   Put some emphasis on a good way to feel about yourself. We all, I think, have our times of getting down around our own feet, despondent, depressed and troubled. Sometimes events and other people can get the better of us, and down we go. And we keep behaving as if that's where we really belong. We let ourselves slip; our dignity slips and our ethics slip. Oh yes, I have had another excursion into the "Modern Guru" page of *The Age* magazine. Humorist Moya Sayer-Jones answered the question of one correspondent whom felt a little guilty for reading all the gossip parts of

somebody else's life. The correspondent said I knew I should not do this, but "I could not stop myself... Did I do the wrong thing?"

Moyer Sayer-Jones wasted no words:

> *"You know you did the wrong thing ... you know that it was no better than reading someone else's diary or eavesdropping on a lovers' squabble. With one fell swoop you turned from quite a nice person with principles into a petty media pervert ... Invest in a good nip and tuck on your ethics now – your principles are getting flabby. And don't stoop to this sort of emotional burglary again."* (17/3/2001)

Notice the cat was not going to lower itself to my level, now that it was up on the fence. We know that he – like all of us – will climb down and compromise himself for a few crumbs or a comforting scratch under his chin. But we know he is more in touch with his highest cat-ness when he climbs on to the high places.

There was a soulfulness about this cat. Soulfulness means being alive to his best possibilities.

3. Put some emphasis on longing for something good and positive.

This cat showed no signs of attention deficit disorder. No signs of succumbing to the ailments of fatigue. The cat had risen to take hold of the day's gift of life's possibility. And in his posture, his bearing, in his eyes and in his looking, there was something of that eternal longing that we have all felt at some stage.

Joseph Addison, the English poet called it, "this longing after immortality". Sigmund Freud saw it as an instinctual force in search of pleasure. Abraham Maslow saw it as the need for contentment; others for life and vitality.

From high up on the constructed fence, surrounded by the trees, oblivious to the passing traffic, undistracted by my approach, this cat was looking beyond everything and through everything.

The Jewish American writer Michael Lerner would probably say he had a "spiritual vision of the world". That means it was something more than longing for a quality of life. It was to experience himself as interwoven with the overall fabric of life. He was part of the fabric and he knew it. His longing was not something to draw back from but something to be affirmed. He was part of the colorful dynamic environment, reaching out to the day's gift and actually being part of that gift.

4. Put some emphasis on being connected to a different energy.

The cat found energy that seemed to move him physically, change him mentally, and elevate him emotionally, and extend him existentially as he became woven into the scenery and at the same time a distinctive element of it. This cat, like all of us, lived many different lives, and yet here it seemed to be particularly at home to itself. Out of our various estrangement and exile experiences, we sometimes find a kind of homecoming to ourselves and we are connected with a different energy.

We discover that we can be affected by chance happenings. We discover that our life may be very much swayed by external people and external events. But we also discover in this inner energy that we have a vital inner locus of control over many aspects of our life.

Nikos Kazantzakis' words –

"Things have the value that we ourselves have the capacity to give them. Everything is blank paper, and we write a foolish or an enthusiastic phrase ... I try to observe the following motto – 'The more value I find in life, the more value I myself have.'" (Kazantzakis p.52)

We are able to get in touch with the part of the self that is home to the self. We can let go our emotional and imaginative imprisonment, and in mind and spirit climb up to the high places – the energy of it.

In Shakespeare's, *All's Well That Ends Well*, Helena speaks words to Parolles, that we might embrace:

> *"Our remedies oft in ourselves do lie*
> *Which we ascribe to heaven: The fated sky*
> *Gives us free scope, only doth backward pull*
> *Our slow designs when we ourselves are dull."*

Religion and the churches, health, psychology and the medical fields have often put emphasis on what has gone wrong with us: on our shortcomings, on our frailties and failings.

I put to you a very significant alternative emphasis, strongly affirmed in the scriptures and urgently needed in every expression of preventive medicine, psychological and emotional health – and a most important part of a relevant religion.

Emphasize:

1. Finding ways to rise above the difficult situation.

2. Finding ways to feel good about yourself.

3. Finding that positive longing for life's best gift and purpose.

4. Finding ways to be connected to a different, vital energy of life.

Get up there with the ginger cat. What did it say? "Everything is different up here."

One Joy Scatters a Hundred Sorrows

H elen Prejean, a nun, wrote the book, *Dead Man Walking*. It is also a film in the cinemas. No one could walk away from the film undisturbed. No one can put the book down unmoved.

Patrick Somnier was on death row awaiting his execution for murder. Helen Prejean was to be his chaplain as he waited –

> *"I am surprised by how human, how likeable he is ... I had half expected to meet Charles Manson – brutish, self-absorbed, paranoid, incapable of normal human encounter."* (p.31)

> *"When I die, I want you to be with me,"* he says.

And so she became such a presence to several men on death row. Asked to visit death row inmates in Louisiana, she became their spiritual adviser. She asked, "Why me?" And the answer came back –

> *"Because they are facing death and your care will make a great difference to them."* (p.117)

Her presence would bring a little softness to the social tragedy of death row.

In our work with people who have been through one or many traumas, we know they are not usually facing death. Many of them are in a peculiar capsule of a living death. We are trying to help them face life and live it differently, hopefully, even enjoyably.

When Jesus of Nazareth rode into ancient Jerusalem, he paused and wept, and said, "You did not recognize God's moment when it came."

There was a presence in your midst and you did not realize the importance of it. You went after your concerns, and things rushed away from you. So Sister Prejean wrote –

> *"I put my hands upon the screen as close as I can get to him and say a prayer ... He bows his head and I find myself looking at the top of the black, knitted hat, which he will give me as a gift ... at the end right*

before he walks to the electric chair ... I ask God to give him what he needs – mercy, courage, remorse for the pain he has caused, and freedom of heart to accept death when he meets it." (p.192)

Some of us in the trauma program have that extraordinary privilege of standing alongside people in their time of upheaval and pain.

A presence – believing that no matter what circumstances brought this pain, tragic events can be softened.

God's moment is the good moment when we recognize the power of such a presence. It is like finding one joy that scatters a hundred sorrows.

II

People caught in the capsule of worry and emotional pain often feel that the whole horizon has gathered in around them. The environment once held some warmth. Now the environment is bleak.

When I was a child living on an isolated farm, there were those times when my parents went off to Bendigo 35 kilometres away to the market or to purchase goods. It would mean a late arrival home for them. My brothers and sisters and I would walk through the bushland to the top of the rise out of the valley to the gate on the driveway. There with the dogs we would wait, swinging on the gate, sitting on the gatepost. The darkness would fall and the distant horizon would become completely black like a heavy black curtain coming in closer to us.

But then, 3 or 4 kilometers away, we would see, coming over the hill, the headlights of the car. Suddenly, the uncertainty and waiting became insignificant, and the whole environment exploded with all of us shouting and dogs barking. For a long period we were stuck with the reality of waiting. But suddenly we were excited by all the new possibilities – "One joy scatters a hundred sorrows."

Often, too often, in our trauma counselling we see the opposite – one sorrow scatters a hundred joys. One tragedy; one death in the family; one word from the doctor; one turn in the road; one misjudgment of behavior – one sorrow scatters all the pre-existing joy.

What we look for is the one joy that scatters a hundred sorrows. Midst all the difficulties or uncertain realities, we get a glimpse of the possible – a light on the dark horizon recognizing the good moments, perhaps God's moment, when it comes.

III

Jesus of Nazareth saw that those people had not got into focus. One minute they were fully with him; the next they would just as happily leave him, and all he stood for.

They could shout, and sing their hymns and psalms, but the next moment, they would turn on him. Just like us.

We can be all over the place. Many fragments. Sometimes we think we have got the pieces together, and then we run out of focus again. Sometimes we think everything is falling apart and life is too dangerous or too capricious, too chaotic or too much in the hands of chance. But then I re-read a little piece of Robinson Crusoe and I hear something important that we do in trauma therapy. We help people edit their realities to make them more manageable. We help them focus their lives once more, so that the dangerous and the distressing thoughts and worries are screened out of their line of vision.

So in Robinson Crusoe, I reflected –

> *"how infinitely good providence is, which has provided in its government of mankind such narrow bounds to his sight and knowledge of things; and*

> *though he walks in the midst of so many thousand*
> *dangers, the sight of which, if discovered to him,*
> *would distract his mind and sink his spirit, he is kept*
> *serene and calm, by having the events of things hid*
> *from his eyes, and knowing nothing of the dangers*
> *which surround him."*

The autumn leaves in the street – they fall in their thousands – and some people get so concerned about them that they are out sweeping them up every day. Yet if they were to wait, one gust of wind would blow them away.

One joy scatters a hundred sorrows!

IV

It is difficult to recognize God's moment when it comes. Is it in this gift, or that relationship? Is it doing this piece of work or going after a different goal altogether? Is it in this surge of happiness or in that search for wealth and fame? Jesus of Nazareth was quite categorical in stating they did not recognize the good moment when it came.

Most people give God's good moment away and pursue their own good moments. How can you believe in God when children die in house fires; innocent, fun-loving, family-loving, backpackers are murdered in cold blood – when bad things happen to good people?

In our trauma work, we are dedicated to one reassurance – tragic events can be softened. Search for it and you stumble on some valid and good consolation. In the turmoil of painful emotions, someone brings you a good feeling. Every time I stand in a hospital ward, I think what a huge difference one or two flowers make to the often bleak experience of looking out the hospital window.

One Friday, after a week that had several lumpy patches, I wandered into a bookshop, and picked up a little book called, *Pooh's Little Instruction Book*, inspired by A.A. Milne. It contains some very worthwhile instructions –

> *"Just because an animal is large, it doesn't mean he doesn't want kindness."*

> *"When you are pretty sure that an adventure is going to happen, brush the honey off your nose and spruce yourself up as best you can, so as to look ready for anything."*

> *"When climbing a tree on the back of a Tigger, be sure to find out before you start if the Tigger knows how to climb down."*

> *"Sometimes a boat is a boat, and sometimes it is more of an accident. It depends on whether you are on top of it or underneath it."*

> *"When someone gives you a bath that you don't really want, one which changes your color, remember that you can roll in the dirt on the way home to get your nice comfortable color again."*

> *"If you've eaten the honey that was meant as a birthday gift for a friend, just wash out the pot and get somebody to write 'A Happy Birthday' on it, and present the pot as a gift."*

With a little book like that, tragic events can be softened a little. And perhaps one joy begins to scatter a hundred sorrows.

V

The good moment. Sometimes it is a moment of transition and transformation. Sometimes we are the bearers of that transition and transformation.

I shall tell you two stories. When I was in Gairloch in the north west of Scotland, I noticed one late afternoon the tide was out, and the many boats were all on their sides. A couple of hours later, I walked out the front door of the hotel and looked down, and those boats were on top of the water. The whole sight was transformed by the wash of the tide.

I try to transfer that imagery into everyday life.

The second story comes straight out of, "A 2nd Helping of Chicken Soup for the Soul."

> *"Bob Harris and wife Tere had driven their new car from Texas to California (their home). They arrived late at night, decided to have a hot shower and get some sleep. They would unpack the car in the morning.*
>
> *In the morning, 'when we opened the front door there was no car in the driveway'. Then, Tere asked this wonderful question, 'Well, where did you park the car?' 'We both knew where we had parked the car, but we both walked out, hoping that may be the car had somehow backed out of the driveway and parked itself by the curb, but it hadn't.'*
>
> *The police, the search. The anxiety, and Tere getting more and more upset because of all the irreplaceable family photographs from past generations, cameras, wallets, cheque butts – all gone.*
>
> *They were items of little importance to our survival. But they became of major importance, then and there. Tere got frustrated and angry, and at length I said – 'Look, we can have a stolen car and be all upset, or we can have a stolen car and be happy. Either way we*

> *have a stolen car. I truly believe our attitudes and moods are our choice and right now I choose to be happy.'*
>
> *Five days later, the car was returned. All of our belongings were missing. Three thousand dollars worth of damage to the car. I take it to the repair dealer and a week later our new car was in my possession again.*
>
> *On my way home, just as I was exiting out of the freeway ramp, I rear ended a car in front of me. At least $3000 worth of damage, but I drove it home, and just as I got out to examine the mess, the front tyre went flat.*
>
> *Tere arrived at that very moment. She saw the state I was in. She said, 'Look, we can have a wrecked car and be upset, or we can have a wrecked car and be happy. Either way, we have a wrecked car, so let's choose to be happy.'"* (p.185-187)

Transitions and transformations. Sometimes they happen right in front of us as I saw at Gairloch. Sometimes they happen because of what our attitude is – we can become bearers of transitions and trans-formations and become part of God's good moment as it comes.

1. A presence.

2. Seeing the possible.

3.   Putting the pieces into focus.

4.   Knowing that tragic events can be softened.

5.   Being part of the transition and transformations.

One joy scatters a hundred sorrows – God's good moment – and we can be part of it!

THE HUMAN SPIRIT

The Big World from the Little Minch

Little Minch is a stretch of water between the Outer Hebrides and the Isle of Skye. Since there is a Little Minch, you would expect there would be a Big Minch. There is! It is simply called, "The Minch" – a much larger stretch of sea between the upper islands of the Hebrides and the mainland of Scotland. It takes four hours to cross the Minch and two hours to cross the Little Minch.

To get our geography right, imagine the British Isles. Scotland sits at the top. Over on the left side, high up on the west coast, there is the port of Ullapool. If you take a boat and proceed for four hours to the left in a north-westerly direction, you'll more than likely run into Stornaway, one of the largest towns in the Hebrides. The Hebrides is made up of an archipelago with six main islands – Lewis, Harris, North Uist, Benbecula, South Uist and Barra.

On my overseas trip, I had eight or nine days to fill in, so I decided that these days would be spent in a place that nobody else would want to go to; hence my decision to go to Lochmaddy on North Uist, far away from everything!

I had already been whirled in the churn of four international conventions of psychologists - in Southampton, Aberdeen, Edinburgh and Vienna. I left Vienna at six o'clock in the morning, with one stale roll and an orange juice for breakfast; flying to London then to Glasgow. By a little mess-up of my travel plans, I then found I had to drive from Glasgow to Ullapool – a distance of 250 miles in five-and-a-half hours. Now that is almost impossible anywhere but particularly so in Scotland. If I missed the boat for Ullapool, that would have meant the end of my trip to the Hebrides for I could only get a booking on this one. My car was the last car to be taken on the ferry at Ullapool.

You have to leave your car in the hold and you are not permitted into the hold again until you reach your destination. I was quite ready to get out of that car, and get a bite to eat, for I had not had a single moment to eat anything since 5.30 am in Vienna. The menu, I was told, consisted of baked beans on toast and steak and kidney pie. I settled for the latter, and then wished I had not. I walked the ship and observed my fellow passengers very carefully – old people with walking sticks; young fellows smoking, drinking and playing cards; young parents shouting at their uncontrollable children – and all of them spread out on every seat available. I had no alternative but to stand, and I took up my position on the promenade deck, port side.

I then made two disturbing discoveries: first, the European summer had not yet reached the Minch, or an early winter had set in. It was wet and freezing cold, and there I was in short sleeves, with what little warm clothing I had, locked in the car in the hold. Four hours of it! Second, I had not reckoned on this journey being like a trip on a roller coaster. The thought of the steak and kidney pie was no longer a happy thought. But I stood my position with resolution on the port side, and so we cut our path through that strong Scottish sea.

Half way across, the people, who had been sprawled over every seat inside, decided to come out and join me in my rocking blizzard. But despite my earlier careful observation of these people, I now found they were all totally unrecognizable. They had all turned green! On that cold night in August, the Minch of Scotland increased its volume considerably.

For the next two days on the islands, we were swept with horizontal rain, and blown to left and right by winds and gales. Lochmaddy Hotel had a blackout. No hot water (not that that mattered, because baths are fairly rare), but I shave electrically and so I began to be a little uncomfortable. "How long will it be off?" I asked. And was told, "Usually not more than four days."

One day I had driven right down the south and in the evening was returning. It was teeming. It was dark; I had become a little uncertain of my direction. A young woman at the roadside reassured me. Now I cannot describe to you how drenched this woman looked. It was as if she had just stepped out from under a bursting 2000-gallon tank. So I said to her, "You are very wet." She made a beautiful statement in return. She opened her toothless mouth (some dentist had a real field day over on the Hebrides because many of them are toothless) and she said, "Oh, it's quite all right, I'm only going to the store."

At many places on the mainland in Britain, as here, when you are driving on the motorways, you come on the sign (that reminds you of your petrol supply), which says, "Last chance to top up for 15 miles." Perhaps it gives you an idea of the remoteness of the Scottish Hebrides when I tell you that when I was passing from north Uist to Benbecula, the only garage

I saw had a huge sign that said, "Last chance to top up for 15,000 miles."

My visit to the Hebrides was one of the most unusual experiences of a lifetime. If I experienced anxiety in getting on to those islands, it was only half the anxiety I experienced getting off them. If the weather becomes too bad, they take the ships off. But on the day I eventually left, the sun was shining, cameras were clicking, the sea was calm and the gulls were doing loop the loop in the wake of the ship – all was forgiven.

II

The conventions I attended in Britain, Europe and America were all gatherings of psychologists from countries so different as China to Africa, Poland to Mexico, Saudi Arabia to Australia, America to Russia, India to Switzerland, and so on.

The major symposia at the conferences were devoted to discussions on the psychology of peace and the ways psychologists could help the urgent movement of peace.

On the last day of the Washington convention, a sunrise service was held at the Washington monument. There, psychologists gathered. Behind on the lawns I noticed hundreds of doves, looking as if they were listening, waiting and wondering if they would be given a message to take to the world. As the sun rose over Washington, the aging B.F. Skinner called on the psychologists present to take action, "lest," he said, "by our own silence we become accomplices to the holocaust".

One of the psychologists (an American Jew) had had several meetings with Yasir Arafat and had tried to see how this man thinks. He had discovered that, unlike the image we often see of him, Arafat was a thoughtful, incisive and generous man, looking for a way to settle a complex situation.

III

Alongside these events in the psychological world, I want to mention events of the church as I saw them. I attended churches in Britain, Europe and America. On one Sunday, I attended three church services – not because I wanted to, but out of sheer professional interest.

In the whole time I was away, I did not hear one sermon that was worth the time I spent listening to it. Every church service I attended was boring as hell and I sweated that people at St Michael's might have the same experience when I am in the pulpit. So I decided there and then that we would begin to make some changes in our services here, lest we become as boring as the services that I endured. With one exception, all the churches I visited were poorly attended – even The Fifth Avenue Presbyterian Church in New York. On my previous visits to that church it had been fairly full. This time it was fairly empty. They had a visiting preacher – no less than a professor of preaching. I thought that here at least I should get a good sermon. It was the worst sermon of all those I heard.

St John the Baptist Church in Perth, Scotland, was once a vigorous colorful church. There were six in the choir and the service was one of despair.

In the Hebrides, once the home of strong free presbyterianism, several of the churches are being used as barns, and one was a machine shop. St Giles Cathedral, Edinburgh, has arranged its seating in such a way as to give the impression of a full church, but only 200 seats are available. The building itself is in bad shape and here, they are looking at a restoration bill of 10 million pounds. They have launched an appeal for the first stage of 800,000 pounds.

Of course there are those who say, "One day there will be a revival in the church and people will return to it." They assume that everything else has stood still.

Take the people of the Hebrides: they will never be the same again. They have crossed the Little Minch. They have crossed the Big Minch: and the world for them is no longer as it was. Television has come. Oil has been discovered. The bomb is not far away, for the island of Benbecula is one of Britain's biggest missile-launching stations. The magnificent beach at Benbecula is starkly marked with signs, "Missile debris may be washed onto these beaches. DO NOT TOUCH. These may kill you."

These people have lived with wars for generations. Scattered across the islands there are monuments to young men of North Uist, South Uist, and Benbecula; men who fought and died in the First World War, the Second War and several others.

It was pouring rain, but I stopped to examine one of the monuments. I was absolutely astounded to see how many young men had gone from these remote islands, and died in war. Names on the east side, west, north and south. Names galore: young men. And then this inscription was written by their fathers and mothers, wives and children:

> *"In three continents and in the deep they lie, but they are in our heart forever enshrined."*

IV

Three Events and Three People

The events:

1. I was in Vienna on Hiroshima weekend (August 6). On the Saturday afternoon, I walked down several streets to take photographs and found myself being swept along in one of the marches to save Europe from nuclear war. I decided to join the march through several streets and then into the large plaza outside St Stephen's Cathedral, where a huge crowd was waiting for the marchers to arrive. Old and young broke into cascades of applause to welcome marchers into the plaza, and they began to sing, "No more Nagasaki, no more Hiroshima, all we want is peace."

2. I stayed a little while at a rather quaint and ancient village called Baden, 20 kilometres outside Vienna. I was fascinated to find that here was Beethoven's summer house and here he wrote the large part of his Ninth Symphony, part of which we sing here in church, "Hymn to Joy".

In the small village church, there was an inscription to Mozart, for here in Baden, Mozart composed for his friend Anton Stoll the "Ave Verum," which our choir at St Michael's frequently sings.

3. The third event proved a rather moving experience when I drove the roads of Scotland. I had never quite experienced the hills of Scotland as I did this time. Instead of simply driving along the road, it was as if I were driving into the hills themselves and as I did so, they seemed to arrange themselves around me. If you ever travel the road through the forests of Athol or between Glen Shiel and Invergary, then you will find the nurturing influence and effects of the hills.

People

1. A man who had recovered from a severe episode of schizophrenia. He was NOT a clergyman, but he gave the best sermon I heard. He was simply talking on television. He told of his serious breakdown and of his recovery, and he added –

    "People take their sanity too much for granted. They throw tantrums and carry on without

realizing what extraordinary things sanity and normality are. Life is so enormously wide and terrific, if you have been given the chance to live it."

2. George Burns, comedian, at the age of 79 became an actor. At age 81 he played the part of God. He said, "I was pleased to play the part of God, and I did it without makeup." "Why shouldn't I play God?" he asked. "Everything I do these days is a miracle! And now, at the age of 86, I am a country singer. That took some doing," he said. "I had to give up sky diving."

3. Winifred Rushforth, a psychoanalyst in Edinburgh. I renewed my acquaintance and visited her in her home. She is 97. She said, "The only thing that's going is my eyes." And then she added, "Did you always have hair as fair as that?" She has written a book in these last important years of her life. In it, she writes:

> *"I have put off writing this book although the urge has been there for many years. I have longed to share what has seemed to be 'good news' — some sort of gospel — with others but have held back till now, my 96th year."*

> *"I have questioned whether I have one thing worthwhile to say, anything that other folk have not said many times. I have, perhaps arrogantly,*

> *wanted to present original truth but now realize*
> *that truth lies deep in the unconscious of each of*
> *us, 'at the bottom of the well', and that it is there*
> *all the time for us if we are willing to go to the*
> *well draw to water."*

The Big World from the Little Minch

In my travels I heard many high-powered papers on changing human behavior; I was deeply affected by the awareness of the terrible prospect of war and the way thousands of people are marching to save the world. I was struck by the mad murder of Ruth First in Mozambique and the abiding sadness of the Glen of Weeping at Glencoe. I was inspired by many things and several people. Although the churches are just a step away from being closed, I saw many excellent examples of how God does not rely on the churches to pass to the world a word of hope, inspiration and joy.

I was fascinated by one of the lochs of the Hebrides close to the North Atlantic Ocean and affected by the tides. When the tide was out the fishing vessels and boats were left stranded in the mud, careened on their sides. Small pools of water remained, but for the most part this section of the loch was empty. But as the tide began to come in, you could hear it coming. You could see it coming. You could smell it coming. The small pools were suddenly brought to life by the flow of the new high tide. The boats were lifted upright and on to a new level. The whole scene dramatically changed from one that was bereft and stagnant to one that was alive with the movement, energy and power that had flowed in with the tide.

As I crossed Little Minch to Skye, the waters were calm, the sun shone through the mist, and there in the sky was a perfect rainbow In the most intense colors: it has always been a symbol of hope: a new beginning. That seemed to be the message of Little Minch to the big world: hope lives on and urgently calls every human being to take hold of it.